Rebaptism Calmly Considered

Rebaptism Calmly Considered

*Christian Initiation and Resistance
in the Early A.M.E. Church of Jamaica*

Sharon J. Grant

FOREWORD BY Ted A. Campbell

☙PICKWICK *Publications* · Eugene, Oregon

REBAPTISM CALMLY CONSIDERED
Christian Initiation and Resistance in the Early A.M.E. Church of Jamaica

Copyright © 2019 Sharon J. Grant. All rights reserved. Except for brief quotations in critical publications or reviews, no part of this book may be reproduced in any manner without prior written permission from the publisher. Write: Permissions, Wipf and Stock Publishers, 199 W. 8th Ave., Suite 3, Eugene, OR 97401.

Pickwick Publications
An Imprint of Wipf and Stock Publishers
199 W. 8th Ave., Suite 3
Eugene, OR 97401

www.wipfandstock.com

PAPERBACK ISBN: 978-1-5326-5299-8
HARDCOVER ISBN: 978-1-5326-5300-1
EBOOK ISBN: 978-1-5326-5301-8

Cataloguing-in-Publication data:

Names: Grant, Sharon J., author

Title: Rebaptism calmly considered : Christian initiation and resistance in the early A.M.E. Church of Jamaica / Sharon J. Grant.

Description: Eugene, OR: Pickwick Publications, 2019 | Includes bibliographical references and index.

Identifiers: ISBN 978-1-5326-5299-8 (paperback) | ISBN 978-1-5326-5300-1 (hardcover) | ISBN 978-1-5326-5301-8 (ebook)

Subjects: LCSH: African Methodist Episcopal Church | Jamaica—Church history—18th century | Jamaica—Church history—19th century | Jamaica—Church history—20th century | Jamaica—History | Missions—Jamaica

Classification: BR645.J3 G71 2019 (print) | BR645.J3 (ebook)

Manufactured in the U.S.A.   AUGUST 27, 2019

[Scripture quotations are from] New Revised Standard Version Bible, copyright © 1989 National Council of the Churches of Christ in the United States of America. Used by permission. All rights reserved worldwide.

I dedicate this book to my parents, Rev. Hector J. Grant Sr. and Ms. Hertha Black Grant, my siblings, and to my paternal aunts, the late Ms. Maysie Grant and Mrs. Hilda Knight Reid. Their love and care for me in Jamaica during this research project are not taken for granted. I am because my village *is*.

Lastly, to the late Bishop Sarah Frances Davis, who still inspires me to pray.

CONTENTS

Foreword by Ted A. Campbell xi

Preface xv

Introduction 1

1. Revival Roots 14

2. Jamaica and Revivalism 27

3. Baptism, the Western Church, and Wesley 59

4. Methodist Missions and Baptist Resistance 77

5. The Allen-Wesleyan Legacy in Jamaica 105

Bibliography 135

Index 143

ACKNOWLEDGEMENTS

I MUST ACKNOWLEDGE PROFESSOR *Emeritus* Richard Heitzenrater for his support during my residencies with the Summer Wesleyan Institute at Duke Divinity School; former Dean William Lawrence and my dissertation adviser Dr. Ted Campbell of Perkins School of Theology for their bedrock support; my current servant-leader, President Vergel Lattimore of Hood Theological Seminary; former colleague President-Dean Ken Walden of Gammon Theological Seminary; and my colleagues at Hood Theological Seminary.

The documents from the African Methodist Episcopal (A.M.E. or A.M.E.) Church Home and Foreign Mission Office are housed at the New York Public Library *Schomburg Center for Black Cultural Studies* in Harlem, New York. I thank Dr. Dennis Dickerson, the former Historiographer and Executive Director for Research and Scholarship, and the generosity of Dr. Diana Lachatanere and her staff when she served at the Schomburg. They permitted me to have access to the uncatalogued A.M.E. documents that contained the written communication between Rev. Alfonso Dumar and Dr. Rankin, the Secretary of Missions, during the early formative years of the A.M.E. Church in Jamaica. Finally, all the churches, clergy, and laity in the A.M.E. Jamaican Annual Conference for their commitment to Wesleyan sanctification and their enduring hospitality to me.

FOREWORD

WHY WOULDN'T THE ARCHBISHOP of Canterbury explain why he baptized Meghan Markle on March 6, 2018, prior to her marriage to Prince Harry? Even popular magazines like *Vanity Fair*, not renowned for its theological depth, got into the speculation.[1] The Duchess of Sussex, as she is now styled, is known to have grown up in a Christian extended family in the United States. The Church of England usually accepts baptisms from other Christian communities. Was she not baptized? Or was she in fact baptized, but in a manner that the Church of England would not recognize? The tantalizing rumor circulated that the Archbishop's act might have amounted to rebaptism. And that's a controversial matter in Christian communities: scandalous, some would say; formally denounced in some churches.[2]

Why would rebaptism be so scandalous? Almost all Christian communities practice baptism as the means instituted by Christ through which believers are incorporated into a Christian community. Rebaptism is a controversial practice because it calls into question the validity of a previous baptism. If, for example, a person was baptized in a Oneness Pentecostal church "in the name of Jesus" only, other churches do not recognize that as a valid baptism, and would "baptize" that person "in the name of the Father and of the Son and of the Holy Spirit," though of course from the perspective of the community that had baptized them in the first place, the second act would be seen as a rebaptism that called into question the validity of the first baptism.[3]

1. Bryant, "Archbishop Who Baptized Meghan Markle Speaks."
2. The African Methodist Episcopal Church explicitly states, "No pastor shall rebaptize" (African Methodist Episcopal Church, *2016 Doctrine and Discipline*, 79).
3. Both the formulae "in the name of Jesus" (Acts 2:38; 19:5) and "in the name of the Father and of the Son and of the Holy Spirit" (Matt 28:19) have explicit grounds in Christian scripture, but only the latter formula is recognized in many—if not most—church

FOREWORD

In this book, Dr. Sharon Grant calmly examines another controversial form of what could be interpreted as rebaptism that carries the implication of questioning the validity and purpose of a preceding water ritual. This is the case, typical of Methodist folk religion in many parts of the world with strong Baptist cultures around them, that the sprinkling of an infant with water using formula, "I baptize you in the name of the Father and of the Son and of the Holy Spirit" is not in fact a baptism but a "christening," and calls for a subsequent act of baptism when that child reaches a point of spiritual maturity and can make a profession of faith form himself or herself. This is not a hypothetical situation: I myself was baptized as an infant in the Rosedale Methodist Church near Beaumont, Texas, in 1953, and then rebaptized at the Memorial Methodist Church in Beaumont in 1963 in association with my confirmation. My parents explained this by saying that the earlier event was a "christening," not really a baptism. This was not formal Methodist teaching, neither in my case nor in the cases of Jamaican Methodist practices examined by Dr. Grant.

In the work that follows, Dr. Grant carefully examines practices of water rituals as they relate to Christian communities of Jamaica in the period leading up to the establishment of the African Methodist Episcopal Church in that Caribbean island nation. She examines not only formal or authorized church teachings and practices, but also the elaboration of these practices in indigenous folk-religious traditions.

But Dr. Grant takes this examination several steps farther, considering the socio-economic settings out of which these practices arose and also considering African cultural traditions that lay in their background. She offers a rich study of interwoven European, African, American, and Caribbean historical and cultural traditions, folk traditions as well as authorized church traditions, as she interprets the practices of baptism, rebaptism, and the broader realm of Christian initiation in the Jamaican cultural background of the early African Methodist Episcopal Church in Jamaica. Her research offers a model for rich, contextual understandings of religious

---

bodies. Speculation about Meghan Markle's baptism by the Archbishop of Canterbury centered around the possibility that she might have been baptized in a Oneness Pentecostal church that baptized her "in the name of Jesus" only, not using the formula "in the name of the Father and of the Son and of the Holy Spirit," which some churches require as constituting a valid baptism. The Archbishop has been careful *not* to state the reason for which he baptized her.

FOREWORD

practices not only among Jamaicans and Methodists, but in broader historical contexts as well.

Ted A. Campbell,
Perkins School of Theology, Southern Methodist University

PREFACE

IN NOVEMBER OF 2009, I travelled to the parish of St. Catherine to interview a Jamaican clergyman and a layperson while conducting field research. I depended upon the minibuses and taxis of the informal Jamaican public transportation system to reach my destination. Once I reached Old Harbour, the largest town in St. Catherine, I looked for the taxis that served the particular district where the A.M.E. Church was located that I was scheduled to visit. After several unsuccessful attempts, I found a taxi man that traveled to and from this district; I asked him if he knew where the A.M.E. Church was and he said yes. Ten minutes or so later, we arrived to the church which he pointed out to me as the "Baptist church." I had been to the church before, so I recognized it, and attempted to correct the taxi driver by saying again, "You mean the A.M.E. church?" He nodded affirmatively and repeated, "Yes, the Baptist church." This exchange reminded me of what prompted my research in the first place.

INTRODUCTION

This project began as a result of my 2003 seminary internship—during which I was privileged to assist the ailing pastor of St. John's A.M.E. Church in Palmers Cross, Clarendon. Near the end of my internship I witnessed a baptism of an adult woman by immersion. As an ordained clergywoman I was familiar with the liturgy read from the A.M.E. Hymnal, but the cultural symbols and interpretive narrative were novel. I found myself fascinated by the effervescent piety of the ritual and began to ask questions about the cultural, sociological and historical forces that shaped the liturgical event I had just witnessed.

In *Main Currents in Caribbean Thought*, Gordon Lewis argues that scholars who attempt to write history with respect to the Caribbean, must note the same forces of "conquest, colonization, slavery, sugar monoculture, colonialism, racial and ethnic admixture" influence each Caribbean country, albeit in differing degrees—and these forces give a particularity to the region as a whole, that distinguish it from mainland societies.[1] This book attempts to describe how these forces combined to shape the doctrinal and liturgical understanding of the practice of Christian initiation in the early years of the African Methodist Episcopal (A.M.E.) Church of Jamaica.

In some respects, the title *Rebaptism Calmly Considered* is misleading, as the tradition being examined is not merely Wesleyan or Methodist but specifically—African Methodist. This distinction is vital for its socio-cultural implications, primarily the African culture(s) that enslaved persons brought with them to the New World; and secondly, the impact of racial prejudice on persons of African descent alongside the imparted meaning of discipleship within congregations of A.M.E. Church. The title is provocative, not the least because the intentional practice of rebaptism

---

1. Lewis, *Main Currents in Caribbean Thought*, 3.

within Methodist denominations is a grave offense that can place offending clerics before their respective judicial committees. Therefore, the Wesleyan phrase, 'calmly considered' follows the controversial noun, to indicate that the aim is a spirited debate supported with ample evidence by both opposing points of view on the subject. As the de facto leader of the people called Methodists, John Wesley ably assumed the responsibility as primary spokesman of the group on matters pertaining to health, sin, wealth, patriotism, and holy living above all.[2]

In eighteenth-century England there was no shortage of polemic religious debate between clergypersons. Two of Wesley's printed publications, *Predestination Calmly Considered*, and *Popery Calmly Considered* reflect the *via media* of an Anglican clergyman who insists upon personal experience, i.e., conversion, church attendance and community service as evidence of authentic Christian discipleship. In the first pamphlet, Wesley's argument presents the merits of humanity's free will against the position of divine election in Calvinism; while in the second, he relies upon Protestant interpretation of Scripture and reason to undermine Roman Catholic doctrine and reliance upon tradition. Further to the point, in his journal and other writings Wesley would often use the phrase 'calmly considered' when recounting the ferocity of gossip and mob activity that prevented Methodists from preaching in many Anglican pulpits as the movement was spreading. See the following excerpt from Wesley's journal entry from 1745:

> The next day, I wrote to a friend as follows: Newcastle-upon-Tyne, March 11, 1745. I have been drawing up this morning a short state of the case between the Clergy and us; I leave you to make any such use of it, as you believe will be to the glory of God. About seven years since, we began preaching inward, present salvation, as attainable by faith alone. For preaching this doctrine, we were forbidden to preach in the churches . . . but we desire any who believes us to preach true doctrine, and has no scruple at all in this

---

2. The desire to attain a practical skill of holy living consumes John Wesley as a young minister and leads him throughout the origin and evolution of the Methodist movement. Wesley describes the growth of Methodism in three stages: first, the Oxford movement, where he organized several Oxford students including his brother Charles in the manner of holy living. The second stage is the Society for the Propagation of the Gospel (SPG) mission that sends John and Charles Wesley to colonial Georgia to serve as ministers to emigrating Brits and evangelize Native Americans. Lastly, the ill-fated mission leads John Wesley to return to England and connect with the Moravians and organize the Fetter Lane Society in London England, the last phase of the Methodist movement that coincides with outdoor preaching organizing classes and commissioning lay preachers.

INTRODUCTION

matter, may not be either publicly or privately discouraged from inviting us to preach in his church. We do not desire that anyone who thinks that we are heretics or schismatic, and that it is his duty to preach or print against us, as such, should refrain there from, so long as he thinks it is his duty. (Although in this case, the breach can never be healed.) But we desire that none will pass such a sentence, till he has calmly considered both sides of the question; that he would not condemn us unheard; but first read what we have written, and pray earnestly that God may direct him in the right way.[3]

This book describes the socio-cultural context that shaped Christian initiation for many early Jamaican congregants within the A.M.E. Church. Christian initiation in early A.M.E. churches included the practice of two water rituals for children within most of its congregations—first, the christening or sprinkling of water on infants, and second, immersion when the child reached the age of consent and made a public confession of faith. At first glance, the use of two water rituals appears to be heterodox, and at odds with Methodist teaching on the sacrament of baptism being performed only once. However, the intent of this book is to present John Wesley's doctrine and practice of the sacrament of baptism alongside the presentation of historical events, social relations and the cultural milieu of nineteenth and early twentieth-century Jamaica to allow the reader to calmly consider the spectrum of evidence to understand how the use of two water rituals became normative for many persons to become full members of the early A.M.E. Church in Jamaica.

The narrative of the African Methodism in the United States and in Jamaica begins with the Evangelical revivals of the Methodist movement in England, and the African cosmology of the enslaved Africans that travelled in the underbelly of slave ships. Born in revival, the Jamaican A.M.E. Church would pride itself on having 'hot worship,' that is a worship experience that invites and implores the Spirit to manifest through exuberance in the song, the dance and the sermon. The exuberance would be especially anticipated during the sacrament of baptism by immersion—the ritual in which a new believer is transferred from the kingdom of darkness into the kingdom of God.

Liturgical expression within the A.M.E. Church in Jamaica includes: the definitive elements of John Wesley's Methodist revival within the

3. Curnock, *Journal of John Wesley*, 168.

REBAPTISM CALMLY CONSIDERED

mid-eighteenth-century Church of England and the communal assent to Richard Allen's egalitarian principles that prompted him to separate from the Methodist Episcopal Church in Philadelphia, Pennsylvania and form the A.M.E. Church. However, new language and symbolism are articulated through the Jamaican socio-cultural experience.[4] The dynamic cross-cultural fertilization process that is unique to the Caribbean is often called *creolisation*.[5] The departed Caribbean scholar Rex Nettleford names it the *Caribbean Experience* and describes it as,

> The organic links of that history/experience with the history of Western Europe and West Africa, with infusions later—much later—from the Orient, the Levantine and post-War America, give to the society of which Jamaica is a prototype, tremendous texture and helplessness. At best it signifies a richness born of the dynamism of a dialectical process in which contradictions battle to forge new synthesis.[6]

This writing seeks to examine the 'new synthesis' of African Methodism that emerged in the crucible of Jamaica's religious and social history. The story, like all stories, revolves around relationships: the relationship between people and those they define as 'other,' most importantly between African people and their God. These relationships spawn a myriad of *thesis—anti-thesis* conflicts resulting in intensely cultural praxis. The century of 1820–1920 is believed by the writer to be most fruitful for observing how cultural history influenced the early Jamaican A.M.E. Church's liturgical practices. It begins with the vigorous anti-slavery climate, which existed just prior to emancipation, and proceeds to the end of World War I along with

---

4. John Wesley, the founder of Methodism, was principally concerned with the evidence of 'scriptural holiness' for persons who identified themselves as Christians. The Wesleyan Revival that began with the outdoor preaching of George Whitefield, John Wesley, and the subsequent formation of Methodist societies is credited (and in turn criticized) with transforming the moral and spiritual lives of many demoralized and impoverished people of England during the early years of the Industrial Revolution. Richard Allen was the founder of the A.M.E. Church and a principal co-founder of the influential *Free African Society*, which stimulated a movement of self-help and dignity among enslaved and freed persons of African descent in Philadelphia, PA during the late eighteenth century.

5. The term was originally coined to describe the Old World's presence or influence in the New World Caribbean colonies. Edward Kamau Brathwaite published *The Development of Creole Society* in 1971, which studied the formation of a local or particular Creole culture.

6. Nettleford, *Caribbean Cultural Identity*, 189.

INTRODUCTION

the emerging Pan-African movement which attained international recognition through the effort of the United Negro Improvement Association, founded by Jamaican National Hero, Marcus Mosiah Garvey. Therefore, this investigation must proceed as an inquiry of the socio-historical events and ideas that shaped persons and personalities in Jamaica who embodied the anti-slavery and pro-slavery factions of the nineteenth century, as well as the colonial and pro-independence factions of the twentieth century. The A.M.E. Church provided a sturdy doctrinal and ideological foundation for African-American communities in North America; yet, most members who would join its churches in Jamaica could not or would not fully assent to the doctrine of infant baptism during the early years of organization and formation in Jamaica, West Indies.

This book hopes to fill in gaps where there is a dearth of scholarly research documenting the historical presence and practices of the A.M.E. Church in Jamaica. Christian initiation has always assumed different forms throughout Christendom, and the exploration of this process in the syncretic model of African Methodism in the Caribbean has the potential of rendering a provocative account of Christian initiation in a unique form with distinctive religious meaning. The studies of African-derived religious traditions have generally focused on the retention of African religion in the New World. There has been little, if any, attention given to the trajectory of the Methodist theological tradition as it expanded through A.M.E. missions in the Caribbean, and particularly as it exists in the witness of the A.M.E. Church in Jamaica.

To accomplish this task, this book interrogates traditional formation of Christian identity, Methodist mission, and the practice of Christian initiation in the early African Methodist Episcopal (A.M.E.) Church of Jamaica. The historical period of 1820–1920 encompasses the nineteenth-century Wesleyan Methodist presence in pre-emancipation Jamaica through the organization of the A.M.E. Church in Jamaica in the earliest years of the twentieth century.

This book provides the academy with an additional description of a religious context shaped in the Black Atlantic, and another narrative of how colonized persons utilized their agency to create a syncretized ritual with African cosmology and a reinterpretation of Christianity to rehumanize themselves in dehumanizing socio-political imprisonment and under crushing economic injustice. Furthermore, and finally, I envision this book being used as a tool to encourage clergy to evaluate the current manner in which the local church prepares candidates for baptism, and the climate in which the performance of the baptismal liturgy occurs. It is my hope that a pastor reading this text will be inclined to evaluate the performance of the baptismal ritual in their local church and reimagine its performance for the edification of participants and witnesses.

A Brief Historiography of Methodism and the Black Atlantic Worldview

The practice of Christian initiation has always been as nuanced as the cultures that inform the beliefs and practices of its people. These cultural distinctions have often fostered competing theological conversations regarding the sacrament of baptism among leaders throughout the Methodist family.[7] In 1958 John Parris published *John Wesley's Doctrine on the Sacraments* and presented the tension that Wesley managed between his Anglican loyalties and his evangelical sensibilities as he considered the place of sacraments in the Methodist movement. Bernard Holland's *Baptism in Early Methodism*, published in 1970, asserted that Wesley believed in two regenerations, the first through infant baptism, and the second by adult conversion. In 1972, Ole Borgen argued against Holland in *John Wesley on the Sacraments*, saying that Wesley only believed in a single instance of regeneration for both infants and adults—which was most often provided at baptism. Gayle Felton's *This Gift of Water* in 1992 offered an account of the theology and baptismal practices of Methodists in North America. Most recently, Ted Campbell, my advisor and mentor published *Wesleyan Beliefs* in which he examines formal and popular expressions of the core set of Methodist beliefs. Pertinent to this study, Campbell offers an account of Wesley's view on baptismal regeneration that analyzes the extent of the Reformed tradition's influence on the Anglicanism that informed Wesley's sacramental theology.

An additional contribution as it relates to Methodism outside of its initial British social context is David Hempton's *Methodism, Empire of the Spirit* published in 2005. Hempton's book is very helpful for examining

---

7. The World Methodist Council is comprised of the Methodist and Wesleyan denominations throughout the globe. The World Methodist Council website states that there are more than 75 million Methodists in the world; World Methodist Council website, "From the General Secretary." Additionally, J. Ernest Rattenbury once stated, "The Methodist beliefs about baptism have always been varied. They certainly are today" (Rattenbury, *Wesley's Legacy*, 193).

INTRODUCTION

Methodism as a transatlantic phenomenon that adjusts and adapts to different geographical and cultural situations, with similar mannerisms that a resilient biological organism might use. Adam Zele's 2008 dissertation, published at Duke University, examines the evolution of John Wesley's relationship with North America throughout his lifetime. This work is useful for building a case for the progression of Wesley's thought on—social ethics, political understanding and theology as related to the United States. This dissertation seeks to build upon the trajectory of Wesleyan thought and research in this descriptive account of the process of catechism and the practice of baptism in many A.M.E. churches in Jamaica.

The ethos that shapes the liturgical practices and theological understandings of the Jamaican A.M.E. Church cannot be understood apart from African traditional religions in the New World and the socio-historical processes of Caribbean creolization.[8] The work of scholars who have done research in these disciplines is expanding rapidly, given the novelty of these fields of study in the academy. John Mbiti's *African Religions and Philosophy* was published in 1970 and provided the academy with general insight into the African worldview. However, Benjamin Ray published *African Religions: Symbol, Ritual, and Community* in 1976 and critiqued Mbiti's excessive generality of African religions.

The scholarship of African religions in the New World is indebted to the work of M. J. Herskovits's *The Myth of the Negro Past*. It was first published in 1941, and was groundbreaking for its affirmation of vibrant African cultural practices throughout the Americas and the Caribbean. Philip Curtin's *Two Jamaicas* was published in 1955, and is an important analysis of the role of ideas on the island. Gordon Lewis's *Main Currents in Caribbean Thought* expands upon Curtin's work and provides a critique of the ideologies that shape the Caribbean worldview; this work came out nearly thirty years after Curtin's in 1983. Charles Long's *Significations*, published in 1986, is vitally important in the work of analyzing a variety of black religious experiences and how they forge a process of meaning-making for enslaved and colonized African peoples in the crucible of the New World. Shirley C. Gordon published two important books, *God Almighty Make Me*

---

8. Although enslaved Africans were brought to Jamaica from diverse geographic regions of the continent, sociolinguistic professor Mervyn Alleyne argues that the Akan tribe of West Africa was most numerous and absorbed other African languages and cultural practices. The syncretism of African spirituality and European Protestant Christianity directly influences A.M.E. churches in Jamaica. See Alleyne, *Roots of Jamaican Culture*, 12.

Free in 1996 and *Our Cause of His Glory* in 1998, both of which address the role of Christianity in the conversion of enslaved Africans and the process of emancipating slaves in Jamaica. Dianne Stewart published *Three Eyes for the Journey* in 2005, as an insightful critique against Christianity, which she names as complicit in the colonial oppression of African traditional religious practices in Jamaica's communities of faith.

Upon review of the recent list of pertinent books it became apparent that within Methodist history and doctrine there are considerable published accounts. Additionally, the discipline of the study of African traditional religions and their influence in the New World is expanding rapidly. Yet, there is a paucity of African Methodist historical accounts and liturgical study in Jamaica and the Caribbean at large. A few scholars are at work to fill this void. This descriptive account of creolized African ritual in the New World asks how did the socio-cultural and religious history of Jamaica from 1820 through 1920, shape communities of faith in the Jamaican A.M.E. Church as they prepared members for Christian discipleship?

This writing narrates the transcontinental phenomenon to demonstrate how a revival may have been experienced by persons of African descent who converted to Christianity in Jamaica during 1820–1920. The revivals of particular importance are the North American revivals commonly referred to as the Second Great Awakening of 1790–1840 and the 1857–58 Revival. The important revivals in the Jamaican religious context are the Baptist Revival of 1860–1861, and the revival associated with the charismatic figure of Alexander Bedward during 1915–1920. The first chapter on revival will necessarily be pneumatologically centered on the work of the Holy Spirit. Methodist doctrine of soteriology rests on how divine grace influences the souls of men and women. John Wesley repeatedly preached about the importance of the 'witness of the spirit' in the lives of persons seeking or claiming conversion to Christianity.

Spirit-possession within African traditional religions offers rich pneumatology, which willingly engages the charismatic strand within the Wesleyan tradition. Enslaved Africans carried this essential trait within themselves when they were transported to the New World, where it would be utilized to validate spiritual connection and self-understanding in ways that European spirituality did not.

Revival in the A.M.E. Church of Jamaica has bifurcated lineage. One line, as argued by Timothy L. Smith, traces its roots to John Wesley as the father of the Protestant revival. The other is rooted in the Native

INTRODUCTION

Baptist revival of 1860-61.[9] The revival of 1860-61 is so significant that a religious movement called Revivalism (or Revival Zion or Revival religion) is named after its influence on the masses of Jamaican peasantry who were members of the Native Baptist churches that experienced the awakening. Diane Austin-Broos and Shirley Gordon effectively argue that the revival of 1860-61 was in fact a progeny of the United States 1857-58 revival.[10] The 1850s period of religious awakening in the United States is often attributed to Charles Finney's evangelistic efforts in New York and Methodist evangelist Phoebe Palmer and her prayer meetings during the 1830s. Soon after, businessmen organized prayer meetings and charismatic worship services emerged which attracted tens of thousands to American churches. "Methodist, Baptist, Congregationalist and New School Presbyterian churches provided most of the lay leadership of the noonday prayer meetings which swept of the cities of America after January 1858."[11] The African Methodist Episcopal Church in North America was a major participant in this evangelical outpouring; eyewitnesses record numerous events of revival preaching by A.M.E. clergy during this time. In response to the evangelical fervor, the nineteenth century became a golden age for missions, and missionary travel was vital for the transmission of ideas from the major metropolitan areas to the colonies. Paul Gilroy's, *The Black Atlantic* describes the processes of modernity, and how new cultures were created by people with 'roots and routes' who travelled between England, Europe and the Americas. While the United States was not yet an imperial power, it was a key producer of Christian missionaries, among which both Baptist and Methodist missionaries would have been influenced by revival.

Within the early Jamaican religious context of revivalism, the converted soul's response to the work of the spirit was communally acknowledged within the baptismal rite. The preferred mode of immersion was ritually concretized in the religiosity of Jamaican revivalism, which is firmly grounded in Native Baptist ecclesiology. Diane J. Austin-Broos's work on Pentecostalism in Jamaica uses the eyewitness account of W. J. Gardner to lay out what she describes as the,

---

9. Native Baptists were independent black churches who ascribed to black leadership, over the leadership of Wesleyan or Baptist missionaries from England. African traditional religious practices and cultural mores were more likely to be retained in these churches.

10. I will use the term "Jamaican religiosity" to refer to the abiding influence of revival religion on the masses of poor persons and persons who live in rural (and urban) areas of Jamaica.

11. Smith, "Historical Waves of Religious Interest," 9-19.

fundamental elements of Jamaica's revival complex as it would be manifest in both Zion Revival and Pentecostalism: *conversion* through the spiritual empowering of possession, *healing* as central in the fight against sin, *foot washing* as a rite of cleansing and *humility* that sustains the cleansing of baptismal immersion, and *strong charismatic leaders* from people constructed by observers as African proponents of sensuality.[12]

The symbolism of the ritual act of immersion was choreographed resistance against oppression as well as retention of memory of ancient West African traditional religiosity.[13]

In what follows, I will attempt to describe the Christian initiation praxis of the Jamaican A.M.E. Church by doing several things. First, in an effort to identify a Wesleyan connection to this descriptive account, I will trace the trajectory of John Wesley's eighteenth-century revival in England through the missionary activity of the Reverend Thomas Pennock, a Wesleyan missionary to Jamaica in the 1820s and 1830s who would eventually publicly renounce his adherence to the efficacy of infant baptism. Pennock is in a minority of early nineteenth-century Wesleyan missionaries who were vocally outspoken against the systematic injustice against blacks and people of color in Jamaica in its civil and ecclesiastical institutions. He served as the District Superintendent at Parade Chapel in Kingston, during the most turbulent period of racial unrest prior to Parliament's passage of the Emancipation Act of 1834. Parade Chapel was a leading, if not *the* leading, church in the Wesleyan Mission to Jamaica, therefore, correspondence from Pennock to the London headquarters will be examined to ascertain the influence of Jamaica's social and cultural climate on his religious worldview.

Secondly, the rite of baptism by immersion will be examined. In an attempt to distil the significance of the ritual, the usage of water in Scripture, the sacraments of the Protestant church, and within selected West African traditional religions will be examined. The ritual of immersion is symbolically important for the A.M.E. Church in Jamaica because of the experience

12. Austin-Broos, *Jamaica Genesis*. 55. Italics mine.

13. Langston Hughes's "The Negro Speaks of Rivers" indicates the importance of rivers on the continent of Africa and their influence on the memory of African descendants throughout the African diaspora. West Africa in particular is filled with rivers and African traditional religion practitioners often associate particular spirits with particular bodies of water. Ritual bathing is very important in several African rites of passage of human development within African Traditional Religions.

INTRODUCTION

of conversion in the life of the baptizand that it represents. Therefore, some attention must be given to the phenomenon of conversion. John Wesley's Christian initiatory practices and his class leader system will be examined to tease out what Randy Maddox refers to as the 'orienting concern.' The work of Thomas Finn and Alan Kreider will be helpful for prompting a depiction of conversion in the Jamaican A.M.E. Church. Finn has studied the ritual dimensions of conversion in various social contexts within the Early Church;[14] while Kreider draws upon Finn's work to explicate a process by which conversion initiates multidimensional change in the life of the believer.

The demonstration of how African culture is retained (to what degree can be, and is argued in Black Atlantic scholarship) in the New World through communal memory will be of paramount importance. Maurice Bloch's work on religion and memory as evidenced through text and oral tradition will be useful, in addition to Jason Young's comparative analysis of religious traditions of pre-colonial Congo and the Low country region of coastal Georgia and South Carolina. In Young's examination, African culture in the Americas is an intentional product of "memory, mediation and creation."[15] It is important to note that the movement of persons and ideas to Jamaica throughout the late nineteenth century was not just one-dimensional, that is moving from the West via North America and England, but that Africans from the continent were also migrating and contributing to the innovative socio-religious milieu of black Jamaican society.

Lastly, the act of immersion and its symbolic link to liberation will be explored in the Jamaican social and cultural context. The precedent set by Rev. George Liele (esteemed founder of the Baptist Church in Jamaica who passed away in 1820), will be set within the narrative of Jamaica's social history of slavery, emancipation, apprenticeship, and colonialism during the 1820–1920 era. The work of Orlando Patterson on the institution of slavery and the concept of freedom will be useful for examining the ideology of Christian egalitarianism and its relationship with civic ideas of freedom and liberty during the early to mid-nineteenth century (i.e., 1820–1850), which precede and follow emancipation. The rise of American imperialism in the late nineteenth century accompanies the rise of the A.M.E. Church involvement with overseas missions. Lawrence Little argues that "Imperialism caused a variety of contradictions, dilemmas, and even paradoxes

---

14. See Finn, *From Death to Rebirth*.
15. Young, *Rituals of Resistance*, 5.

REBAPTISM CALMLY CONSIDERED

for A.M.E. leaders, and although it was impossible to reconcile American ideology with American racism, A.M.E. leaders helped broaden the concepts of liberty and equality within and, with imperialism, beyond American society."[16] The founder of the African Methodist Episcopal Church in Jamaica, the Rev. Alfonso Dumar, brought a gospel of racial egalitarianism and uplift that was received positively by many Jamaican independent congregations during the early twentieth century.[17] However, the Jamaican religiosity of the masses who were drawn to Dumar's 'good news' of racial equality in African Methodism, were largely non accepting of the doctrinal mandate which recognized infant baptism as fundamental teaching of the church.

Dianne Stewart's scholarship confronts oppressive forms of Christianities in Jamaica and North America and demonstrates how African culture and religiosity has been marginalized by Eurocentric Christian hegemony. The response of the marginalized to the dominant culture is at the center of this project. An effective description of the liturgical ritual requires an examination of the historical relationship between the powerful and the powerless within Jamaican Christian communities of faith. Postcolonial scholars Walter Mignolo and *border gnosis*, Homi Bhaba's *hybridity*, and Joerg Rieger's articulation of how the Western Church has been complicit in the colonization of 'the other' provide useful concepts for this task.[18]

Ultimately, this work must address the continuities and discontinuities of Wesleyan thought within the liturgical baptismal ethos of the A.M.E. Church of Jamaica. Without question, John Wesley's enculturation as an eighteenth-century British Anglican priest would have caused him to take pause, if not outright offense at charismatic phenomena that often emerged during worship services led by black preachers and which peaked during the 1861 Jamaican revival. However, Wesley's pragmatic bent was firmly committed to creating communities of faith in which conversion would occur and where converts could be nurtured to maturity. I argue that the trajectory of Wesley's pragmatism is expressed within the baptismal practices of the early A.M.E. Church in Jamaica as it was informed by the

16. Little, *Disciples of Liberty*, xiii.

17. The early mission of the A.M.E. Church to Jamaica was formally acknowledged by the government of Jamaica with the work of W. B. Pearson in 1900. The Jamaica Mission Conference became officially organized under Dumar, and recognized by the connectional church in 1914.

18. See Mignolo, *Local Histories/Global Designs*; Bhaba, *Location of Culture*; Rieger, *Opting for the Margins*.

INTRODUCTION

sociohistorical forces of Jamaican society. The cultural distinctions contributed by the retention of traditional African religion in the social history of Jamaica, ebb and flow within familiar tensions that often challenge Methodism, whenever and wherever it exists.

The methodology employed for this project is not conventional. The *Les Annales School* of historical thought which originated in the early twentieth century with French historians could be viewed to undergird much of what is presented here. Historians who are influenced by this school of thought assume that history should not be limited to merely recording the past results of conscious human action.[19] Instead, *Les Annales* historians insist that history must be recorded in the context of cultural, historical, anthropological and sociological forces which inform human behavior. It will be helpful for the reader to consider this perspective as the central hypothesis of this study is presented and supported by empirical data that reflects the 1820–1920 timeframe in Jamaica. Extensive use of missionary correspondence from the Wesleyan Methodist Missionary *Society* (WMMS) as well as the missionary journal of the A.M.E. Church, *Voice of Missions*, are important documents which provide historical information on social relations, political perceptions and theological questions which shape Jamaican culture. The WMMS documents revealed the social relations between the Wesleyan missionaries, the planter class, and the enslaved Africans were conducted as the work of evangelism and religious instruction of the converted slaves progressed. Letters from the different A.M.E. Secretary of Missions and A.M.E. missionaries in Jamaica provide eyewitness accounts of the issues that early A.M.E. missionaries in Jamaica faced at the turn of the century.

Extant local newspapers from the period were examined to grasp the minutia of pre- and post-slave society. They presented anti-slavery debates and other matters of controversy among the British colonial representatives, local planters, missionaries, and the population of freed blacks and mulattos. The *Jamaica Watchman* and *The Courant* were important nineteenth-century periodicals which featured the work of Wesleyan missionaries in Jamaica. The archives of the *Jamaica Gleaner* have been vitally important for its early twentieth-century account of the formation and organization of the A.M.E. Church on the island of Jamaica.

---

19. In 1929, Marc Bloch and Lucian Febvre founded the *Les Annales School*, which utilized social scientific theory within its historical methodology. See Bloch, *Historian's Craft*; Febvre, *New Kind of History*, 27–43.

Chapter One

REVIVAL ROOTS

By and large, it was the hunger for revival of the soul that motivated the thousands of persons to gather to hear George Whitefield, and later, John Wesley preach. The crowds were a mixed multitude of persons of eighteenth-century British society. They were largely poor and uneducated, yet a few wealthy and intelligent were counted among those who heard the open-air preachers, and the outdoor congregation listened as mockers, skeptics, and well-intentioned seekers. The hunger was caused by a void of religious fervor, which had been largely stifled by Enlightenment ideology. Alongside important continental writings was John Locke's anonymously published, *The Reasonableness of Christianity*, which argued for a liberal, rational form of Christianity and appealed to many clerics within the Church of England. Another matter was the fecundity of scientific experimentation, which challenged the role of divine revelation, such that Deism became a popular alternative to traditional Christianity.[1] In this sensitive climate, religious enthusiasm became perceived as a vice for persons whose memories were still raw from events which caused so much bloodshed on the continent of Europe as well as Charles I's regicide during the English Revolution. With the subsequent defeat of the Puritans and the onset of the Glorious Revolution, political and spiritual tolerance was achieved through rational, thoughtful forms of religion. In this context, rational religious expression became the dominant perspective of the Church of England, its clerics, and its universities, Oxford and Cambridge.

1. Starkie, "Contested Histories of the English Church," 335–51.

REVIVAL ROOTS

The moral laxity, ignorance of the masses and social and economic injustice of eighteenth-century England challenged the effectiveness of the "religion of the head" embraced by the Church of England.[2] As a result, the charismatic preaching of George Whitefield was eagerly received by a hungry audience starving for emotive displays, which addressed their circumstance and stirred their "religious affections." Wesley personally understood the limitations of a religion of the head, having been baptized and ordained before he experienced a profound visitation of the Divine at a society meeting at Aldersgate, on May 24, 1738. He would record in his journal that this experience provided the grounds for trust in God's forgiveness of sin, through the sensory evidence that "my heart was strangely warmed." As a result, under his watch, religious experience was kindled and stoked in the Methodist movement, which began as the ember of the Methodist Revival. The open air meetings were dynamic events as persons across class and station landed in one area, "thieves, prostitutes, fools, people of every class, several men of distinction, a few of the learned merchants, and numbers of poor people who had never entered a place of worship assembled in these crowds and became godly."[3]

Persons in the crowds who affiliated with the Methodists did so by means of joining its Society.[4] Whitefield had loosely organized religious societies in Kingswood and Bristol, however, as the societies grew in size and number, the problem of organization and leadership had to be confronted. The only condition of membership of the Societies was "the desire to flee from the wrath to come." However, this desire was to be made evident through accountability, and accountability required intimacy and reliable leadership. The large crowds at the revival became manageable and accountable through the formation of smaller groups called "classes." The Methodist Society Class was the brainchild of a man named as Captain Foy, created to solve the fundraising problem of finding money to purchase the first Methodist preaching house in Bristol. To alleviate the burden on the

---

2. Plumb, *England*, 44–45. Plumb describes an Anglican church severely weakened by corruption.

3. Johnson, *Frontier Camp Meeting*. 24. Quotation originally found in McTyeire, *History of Methodism*, 154–57.

4. After Parliament passed the *Act of Toleration* in 1689, the Church of England allowed dissenting ministers and congregations to worship after they registered their meeting houses and became licensed. Wesley never allowed the necessity to register the meeting locations of Methodist Societies, because he never considered them as separate entities from the Church of England.

members of the society, who were mostly poor people, Foy suggested that the Society should be divided into groups of eleven under a leader who would collect a penny a week from each person. The classes would be led by laity who reported to John and Charles Wesley who served as the itinerate preachers for the Methodist societies. When Methodist societies evolved into Methodist churches in North America and the Caribbean as a result of missionary efforts, the class leader served as the primary resource person for determining and informing the pastor when inquirers were ready to become candidates for baptism and thus enter into full membership of the church.[5]

The Messenger

"Like many other aspects of early Methodism, lay preaching evolved more out of necessity than design."[6] The emergences of many heralds of the good news in the Methodist evangelical revival were unlike Whitefield and the Wesleys in one major way: they were unordained, lay preachers. The success of the Methodist revival was its pragmatic flexibility. As the organization of Methodist societies became too cumbersome for John Wesley and Charles Wesley to serve effectively, persons who possessed leadership ability and spiritual discipline were nurtured and encouraged to "exhort" in the absence of clergy. Methodist classes thrived when effective laypersons were identified and allowed to lead; and a more intimate group, the "band," was designed to facilitate persons who longed for deeper spiritual maturity. Without capable lay leadership, the early Methodist organizational structure would have suffered great difficulty.

Lay preaching emerged in the Methodist revival as early as 1740. Notable among the early lay preachers was Thomas Maxfield, a committed layman who came to faith in a very emotional way under John Wesley's preaching, and he often accompanied Charles Wesley when he was itinerating. Because of Maxfield's reliability, the Wesleys often entrusted him with leadership responsibilities over society meetings. When it was reported to John Wesley that Maxfield had begun to preach during the gatherings,

---

5. Kevin Watson's *The Class Meeting: Reclaiming a Forgotten (and Essential) Small Group Experience* is an appeal to return to this early Methodist practice and use of Wesleyan spirituality to energize congregants who want to engage in a disciplinary practice of spiritual formation. See Watson, *Class Meeting*.

6. Heitzenrater, *Wesley and People Called Methodists*, 113.

rather than just simply exhort, Wesley was cautioned against reacting too harshly against the irregularity by his mother, Susanna Wesley. "Take care what you do with respect to that young man, for he is as surely called of God to preach, as you are. Examine what have been the fruits of his preaching, and hear him also yourself."[7] John Wesley heard Maxfield and conceded that his mother was correct in her assessment of his gifts and grace. Although Charles never warmed to the idea of the preaching office being inclusive of laity, he yielded to John's leadership in the matter. This concession opened the gate wide for lay leadership in the Methodist movement.

> What happened in the Class Meetings must have varied from place to place, time to time and leader to leader; but the leader was normally a layman-that is, he was neither an ordained clergyman nor a Methodist itinerant preacher—and very often of humble origin and little or no education.... Classes for women were separate from those for men, and for this reason women class leaders played an important part from the start.[8]

The Message

The substantial content of the preaching during the Methodist Revival was evangelical, following John Wesley's admonition to young preachers that they had "nothing to do but save souls." The A.M.E. Church of Jamaica would continue to adhere to this fundamental evangelical premise of the purpose of preaching.[9] John Wesley was a well-read Oxford scholar who was attracted to—and theologically influenced by—Christian thinkers across eras and cultures throughout the Christian world who were ultimately concerned with heartfelt piety.[10] Ted Campbell's work has demonstrated that while the early Methodist movement emphasized a religion of the heart, this affective movement did not occur in isolation—but moved wherever people did during the eighteenth century. The European continent, the

---

7. Green, *John Wesley*, 111–12.
8. Davies, *Methodism*, 73.
9. This emphasis continues in the twenty-first century. When visiting a local Jamaican A.M.E. church in 2010, I overheard an older woman in the congregation urging a young preacher to "preach repentance and get souls saved."
10. Martin Marty utilizes the phrase "the Christian world" to indicate "all the contexts to which Christian believers related and relate" (Marty, *Christian World*, 3).

REBAPTISM CALMLY CONSIDERED

British Isles and their colonies in the New World would not escape the attraction of pietism and its piety with demonstrable religious affection.[11]

Wesley's theological mentors were an eclectic group which included: Greek Fathers of antiquity; monastics; the Moravians and other European Pietists; Puritan leaders and Anglican writers who all shared a concern for heartfelt religious piety. These varied contributions to Wesley's theology provided raw material for a Methodist message which was fundamentally soteriological and affective. Within the revival context, the message was orally presented with the sole intention to stir the emotions of the hearers and generate spiritual hunger for the transforming power of God in the listeners. Thus, the revival service was foremost designed to ensure that sinners heard the message of the atoning work of Christ.

> For example, in preaching to unrepentant sinners, John Wesley spoke of the claims of the divine Law and the certainty of judgment, eliciting reverence for the Law and appropriate fear of divine judgment. In preaching to sinners who had repented but were yet unconverted, Wesley spoke of the promises of God and joy in the thought of forgiveness.... The range of emotions elicited in his sermons is huge and Wesley developed an elaborate vocabulary—specialized taxonomy-to describe this range of affective responses to the gospel.[12]

The previous quote confirms the logic wherewith Wesley would urge his preachers to preach the Law first and then follow with the gospel. The gospel message illustrated the gift of divine grace to sinful humanity in the Person of Jesus Christ. However, this gracious gift had to be accepted and received by faith in order for salvation to be effective. Faith was preached until individuals could have certainty and confidence that Christ died for *their* sins. Revivals aimed to provide assurance to sinners, doubters and skeptics alike. These epistemological considerations, which pertained to knowledge of the divine provided boundaries for the carriers of the message. Charles Wesley, the brother of John Wesley and composer of over seven thousand hymns, utilized his gift of poetry to assure that it served the "greater end of piety" within the Methodist renewal movement. Consider the lyrics of the beloved Methodist hymn, "And Can It Be That I Should Gain?"

> And can it be that I should gain

11. Campbell, *Religion of the Heart*.
12. Campbell, "Way of Salvation," 83.

An interest in the Saviour's blood?
Died He for me, who caused his pain?
For me, who Him to death pursued?
Amazing love! How can it be
That thou, my God shouldst die for me!

He left His Father's throne above
So free, so infinite His grace
Emptied Himself of all but love,
And bled for Adam's helpless race,
Tis mercy all, immense and free;
For, O my God, it found out me![13]

The gospel, as preached in the revival, was rooted in deep personal understanding and knowledge of the nature and actions of God incarnated in and through Jesus Christ. "It was not only that Christ was savior of all; he was the savior *for me*."[14] This message of salvation with the remission of sin proclaimed in sermon and in song stirred the emotions and motivated the will of individual persons to respond to the divine invitation for a transformed life in Christ. The process of being consciously aware of one's identity as a sinner was profoundly disconcerting and initially caused tremendous anguish. When revival congregants sought relief from the blistering knowledge of their sinful condition, spiritual anxiety would often simmer into a cathartic response with dramatic emotional display. The early A.M.E. Church in Jamaica emphasized preaching that intentionally used graphic imagery and emotive content to prick the human consciousness and stir the religious affections of its hearers.

The Response

The dramatic emotional display of some of the early Methodists was labeled enthusiasm by opponents to the charismatic revival occurring outside the

---

13. African Methodist Episcopal Church, *Hymnal*, 459. The lyrics of this hymn were written by Charles Wesley (1707–1788) and *The Bouquet* melody was written by Thomas Campbell (1777–1844).

14. Ruth, *Early Methodist Life*, 32. Ruth states that this personal awareness was transmitted in acts of discipleship, worship, and evangelistic efforts, not formal systematic theological effort. Revivals are typically concerned about personal conversion and social holiness, not academic treatises.

established Church of England. Both John and Charles Wesley were somber Anglican priests who abhorred dramatic emotionalism; however, their respect for the Holy Spirit's *modus operandi* in the lives of believers allowed semblances of heteropraxis when Methodists gathered together for worship. Charles Wesley was the more conservative of the two Wesley leaders of the early Methodist movement and several of his journal recollections during 1739 are useful for determining the character, shape, and tone of the emotional responses as observed by the one of its preeminent leaders:

> Mon. March 12th. . . . I expounded at Bray's on the day of judgment. The power of the Lord was present to wound. A woman cried out as in an agony. Another sank down overpowered. All were moved and melted, as wax before the fire.[15]

> Sun. April 1st. . . . I prayed at Fetter-lane, that the Lord might be in the midst of us; received a remarkable answer. B. Nowers, in strong pangs, groaned, screamed, roared out. I was not offended by it, nor edified. We sang and praised God with all our might.[16]

> Tues. May 1st. . . . Mr. Stonehouse preached a thundering sermon. . . . A poor harlot was struck down by the word. She and all, were melted into tears, and prayers, and strong cries for her. I have a good hope this brand will also be plucked out of the fire.[17]

> Thur. May 24th. J. Bray took upon him to reprove me for checking the course of the Spirit. I made him no answer; but I believe not every spirit; nor any till I have tried it by the fruits and the written word.[18]

These entries illustrate that persons often responded to the Methodist message with tears, sinking down, crying aloud and emotional exuberance through prayer and song. Charles Wesley's pastoral response to each of these emotional events is characterized differently: the first with *approval*; the second with *indifference*; the third with *expectation*; and the final entry does not list what responsive activity prompted the "checking of the course of the Spirit" but whatever transpired warranted *rebuke* in Charles Wesley's estimation. The last sentence in the last entry seems to provide the criteria

---

15. Wesley, *Journal of Charles Wesley*, 144.
16. Wesley, *Journal of Charles Wesley*, 146.
17. Wesley, *Journal of Charles Wesley*, 149.
18. Wesley, *Journal of Charles Wesley*, 150.

REVIVAL ROOTS

by which the poetic priest would evaluate emotionalism—*fruits* and *the written word*.

"Fruits" is an obvious biblical reference to the fruit of the Spirit described in the fifth chapter of the Pauline epistle to the Galatians. Charles Wesley's Anglican inclination as informed by the empiricism of the Enlightenment provides him with the impetus to support every religious decision with scriptural evidence. Emotional outbursts that mocked the message or lacked scriptural verification were to be rebuked. Displays of emotion that reflected repentance and affirmation to the message were to be affirmed and those demonstrations, which neither edified nor offended, were not addressed; but, left to God to determine their usefulness. The expectation of the work of salvation is what is most important. The purpose of the revival was to bring the sinner to belief in the atonement of Christ. Thus, when Charles Wesley speaks of his "good hope this brand will also be plucked out of the fire," he is acknowledging the gracious activity of God, which will transport a sinner from the universal position of prevenient grace to the particular position of justification through an active faith in the atoning work of Jesus Christ.

The context, messenger, and message of the revival provided the kindling for the flame of faith to be kindled in the soul of the convicted sinner. Conviction was often noted and recorded as spiritual awakening or the point at which the sinner became conscious of his or her sinfulness individually, rather than merely the unfortunate plight of humanity in general. John Wesley's sermon, "Awake Thou That Sleepest," intentionally includes a series of inquiries to nudge an unbeliever into alertness.

> Art thou . . . lost, dead, *damned already*? . . . Art thou "poor in spirit," mourning for God, and refusing to be comforted? . . . O that in all these questions ye may hear the voice that wakes the dead; . . . now, "awake thou that sleepest; in spiritual death." . . . Leave thine old companions in sin and death.[19]

Richard Allen's autobiographical testimony recounts his initial awareness of his sinful condition after hearing a Methodist preach. "I was upwards of twenty years of age, during which time I was awakened and brought to see myself poor, wretched and undone, and without the mercy of God must be lost."[20]

19. Outler and Heitzenrater, *John Wesley's Sermons*, 91.

20. Allen, *Life*, 5. Allen was converted in 1777 and was among the first generation of Americans converted to Christianity by Methodist circuit riders.

REBAPTISM CALMLY CONSIDERED

The potentiality and likelihood of losing one's essential self, brought many people to the point of distress. Conversely, the realization that one could be rescued from the eternal consequences of sin would bring about euphoria. The contrasting poles of distress and euphoria in the self are what animate much of the worship in the contemporary Jamaican African Methodist Episcopal Church.

These conspicuous episodes were magnified by Methodism's opponents as points of ridicule and condemnation. The Wesley's were reproved as "grand enthusiasts" and "madmen" who encouraged the noisy and nonsensical behavior of the poor, unruly, and ignorant. Sidney G. Dimond's *The Psychology of the Methodist Revival*, published in 1926, employed modern psychological theory to defend the exceptional psychic/physical phenomena which often occurred. Dimond analyzed the responses of revival participants using the observations in the journals of the Methodist leaders and described them with psychological terminology such as primary instincts, "instinct experience," and crowd behavior. However, the upshot is that Dimond concluded that the revival's influence was useful and provided social value for the improvement of the individual and the betterment of English society.[21]

The Methodist revival was an event initiated by Anglican clergy under the inspiration of the Holy Spirit to evangelize the least, last, and lost in their society. It was implemented with masses of inspired men and women who participated in word, songs and deeds in an effort to "flee from the wrath to come." Lycurgus Starkey reaffirms John Wesley's account of the inspiration of the Holy Spirit as "the main doctrine of the Methodists" and describes the nature of divine inspiration as being perceptible, immediate, uniquely redemptive, and available to all.[22] Perceptibility necessarily involves conscious awareness of the sensation of the work of the Holy Spirit on the spirits of repentant men and women. The immediacy of this awareness, and the various ways in which men and women responded, allowed for tens of thousands of spirited people to revisit the experience of Pentecost within the incendiary setting of *sight, sound* and *response* which characterized the Methodist revival.

---

21. Dimond, *Psychology of Methodist Revival*.
22. Starkey, *Work of Holy Spirit*, 17–21.

REVIVAL ROOTS

The Revival expands to the British colonies

David Hempton explains the adaptation and expansion of the British Methodist movement into a transnational phenomenon, by using the concepts, *competition,* and *symbiosis* from the field of evolutionary biology. According to Hempton, Methodism expanded within the United States because the history of the early republic was amenable to the populist, egalitarian and anti-Calvinist sentiments of its message.[23] As Methodism crossed the Atlantic Ocean to expand into the colonies of Britain, the Methodist preachers had to compete with missionaries of other denominations, the established Church of England, and the religious beliefs and practices of the indigenous populations. African Methodism, the prodigy of the North American Methodist church would also face similar competition when it would establish a missional presence in Jamaica near the turn of the twentieth century.

Methodist societies were first established outside of Britain on the Caribbean island of Antigua in 1759. Its adaptation to its new tropical environment was with relative ease because its founder, Nathaniel Gilbert, was a socially respectable lawyer, politician, and sugar estate owner. After his death in 1774, the religious society seemed destined to fail; however, the leadership void was ably filled by two enslaved women who had been converted with him in England.

> West Indian Methodism must ever preserve the names of "a Negress and a Mulatto," Sophia Campbell and Mary Alley. These devoted women kept the flock together after the going of the Gilberts, carrying on class meetings and prayer meetings as best they could. Their humble and effective work preserved Methodism in extinction in the islands, and they were the forerunners and prototype of the great company of West Indian Class Leaders who have been the back bone of West Indian Methodism ever since.[24]

The Rev. Dr. Thomas Coke, revered as the Father of Methodist missions, officially organized the Methodist Church within the former North American colonies in 1784.[25] Although John Wesley had empowered Thom-

---

23. In addition to the egalitarian message, the antislavery rhetoric and the class leader system of early Methodism made it attractive for enslaved blacks in the United States during the eighteenth and nineteenth centuries. As the plantation societies expanded in the South, white resistance would insist upon racial separation.

24. Methodist Church in Jamaica, *For Ever Beginning,* 15.

25. Coke went to the United States of America with Wesley's guidance and

as Coke with authority to ordain Asbury and other American Methodist preachers, Francis Asbury was already the *de facto* leader of the Methodist leader in the newly formed, fiercely independent republic. Francis Asbury, American Methodism's first bishop, was simply a lay preacher when he answered John Wesley's appeal for help in the North American colonies. He arrived in 1771 and never returned to England. Asbury astutely understood and assented to the revolutionary sentiment of the colonists and aligned the American Methodist church with its democratic principles. Under his leadership, American Methodism became identified with the camp meeting, North America's evangelical response to rugged life on the frontier.[26]

> Bishop Francis Asbury, who had played such an active role in the forest revival's formulative period, remained one of its staunchest advocates, which perhaps accounts for the fact that the open-air revival maintained its influence among Methodists long after other major denominations had stopped using it. Asbury spoke for himself as well as for his co-workers when he declared, "The Methodists are all for camp-meetings; the Baptists are for public baptizings."[27]

The ecstatic behavior which was relatively isolated on the British Isles would become commonplace during the early North American frontier camp meetings. Richard Allen, the founder of African Methodism in North America, began his ministry as a lay preacher in typical Methodist fashion. He was converted in a Methodist gathering and, after being licensed to preach, would become the first man of African descent to be ordained deacon by Francis Asbury before departing the Methodist Episcopal Church.[28] Richard Allen explains in his biography why he purposed to remain Methodist in spite of experiencing humiliation and racial oppression within the

permission. The Methodist societies were initially formed by Irish Methodist clergymen who migrated to the North American colonies in the 1750s.

26. The American camp meeting was an outdoor revival that featured numerous preachers and spontaneous, improvisational prayer and singing. The attendees normally had to camp out near the makeshift worship area, as there were no permanent dwellings in the virgin frontier forestry of North America during the late eighteenth and early nineteenth centuries.

27. Johnson, *Frontier Camp Meeting*, 82. Johnson cites Asbury's quotation from an entry of October 21, 1810, in Asbury, *Journal of Rev. Francis Asbury*, 349.

28. Allen was ordained in 1799. He and another black Methodist preacher—"Black Harry" Hoosier—were present at the 1784 Christmas Conference in America, however there is no record of Hoosier ever being ordained.

REVIVAL ROOTS

St. George's Methodist Episcopal Church congregation of Philadelphia, Pennsylvania.

> I was confident that there was no religious sect or denomination would suit the capacity of the coloured people as well as the Methodist; for the plain and simple gospel suits best for any people, for the unlearned can understand, and the learned are sure to understand; and the reason that the Methodist is so successful in the awakening and conversion of the coloured people, the plain doctrine and having a good discipline.[29]

The attraction of the "plain and simple gospel" to which Allen speaks summarizes the impact of the evangelical message that revival preachers in the fledgling republic were expected to deliver. The successful revivalist possessed the ability to influence the learned and the unlearned alike by appropriating the message and utilizing the gifts of elocution and charisma. This was especially important for the new African converts to Christianity.

Thomas Coke continued to expand the presence of Methodism as its first missionary. The West Indies were the next priority for the man John Wesley once called "the flea" because of how he "hopped" from place to place in overseas mission activity. Coke ably assisted John Wesley in his later years with the pressing demands of an expanding Methodism outside the boundaries of Britain. Coke's first of six mission trips to the West Indies was marked by providence in late 1786. Wesley's guidance and the mandate of the Conference directed Coke to respond to requests for missionaries in Nova Scotia and the West Indies. The plan was for Coke to travel to Nova Scotia to install two missionaries—John Clarke and William Hammett, and then proceed to Antigua with a third, William Warrener. However, a terrible storm blew the ship some 2,000 miles off course and all four landed on the island of Antigua on the Christmas morning of 1786. Coke would return to the Caribbean in the autumn of 1788, and during this journey, he organized missions in Barbados, Dominica, Nevis, the Virgin Islands, and Jamaica.

After a few days he secured venues to commence preaching, initially in a private house, then afterwards a gracious Roman Catholic granted him the use of a large hall. On the second evening of his preaching Coke experienced firsthand the rough behavior of those opposed to Methodist preachers. As he preached to a congregation of about 600 persons, a group of inebriated white men interrupted the meeting with shouts of "Down

29. Allen, *Life*, 15.

with him, Down with him," and attempted to seize him. A large disturbance followed, after which members of the congregation came to the defense of Coke and placed the drunken gang on the defensive. With this introduction to the gospel, as preached by a Methodist, Jamaica quickly developed and maintained its reputation for being the most difficult assignment in the West Indies for Methodist missionaries. Nevertheless, Coke persevered long enough to organize the first Methodist class in Jamaica before he left. William Hammett, who arrived in August 1789, became the first Methodist missionary to Jamaica.

The Methodism established in Jamaica was initially accomplished by British Wesleyan Methodist missionaries. This distinction becomes important along the Methodist trajectory of missionary expansion; because, while Wesleyan Methodism and American Methodism are similar in substance, they are dissimilar in character and tone. By the time of John Wesley's death in 1791, Wesleyan Methodism had acquired considerable social respectability. Furthermore, the leadership style of Jabez Bunting in the nineteenth-century British Methodist Church muted the emotionalism of the eighteenth-century Methodist revival. Expressions of religious ecstasy were frowned upon in England, while in North America, Francis Asbury and his frontier preachers nurtured pietist impulses into emotional content within the camp meetings that typified early nineteenth-century American Methodism. American Methodism's protégé, the African Methodist Episcopal (A.M.E.) Church would begin to send missionaries in the late nineteenth-century to Jamaica, where John Wesley and Richard Allen's legacy emerged in a unique church, which utilized competition and symbiosis within a context of vigorous resistance to oppression and effervescent popular religiosity.

Chapter Two

JAMAICA AND REVIVALISM

The emotional expression of the Methodist revival was particularly attractive to Africans who would convert to Christianity in both North America and Jamaica during the eighteenth and nineteenth centuries. The emotive content of early Methodist worship services dove-tailed alongside the normative phenomena of spirit possession within most traditional African religion as practiced by enslaved Africans in the 1700s and 1800s.

In response to various charismatic phenomena by certain members, leaders within the Church of Allen would wrestle between the notions of religious respectability and expressive piety.[1] This distinction has been highlighted in the work of Bishop Frederick Hilborn Talbot. Talbot argues that the A.M.E. Church has continually wrestled with tensions within two contrasting liturgical styles as exemplified in the dual personalities of Bishop Richard Allen and Bishop Daniel Alexander Payne.[2] Richard Allen was an unlearned, self-taught freedman who had to overextend himself to purchase his freedom. He preached with emotional fervor and encouraged the singing of hymns and choruses to stir up expressions of piety within his congregation. Conversely, Payne (elected the sixth Bishop of the A.M.E. Church in 1852) was born to freed parents and was given every opportunity to become educated. Before he became an A.M.E. minister, Payne was granted an offer to study at Gettysburg Theological Seminary in Pennsylvania, which he accepted, and also pastored a Presbyterian Church in

---

1. The Church of Allen is another way of identifying the African Methodist Episcopal Church.

2. Talbot, *African American Worship*.

REBAPTISM CALMLY CONSIDERED

New York. Payne possessed a sober demeanor and demanded respectability and decorum in worship services. He insisted upon education for ministers and was the progenitor of the Course of Study for the clergy of the A.M.E. Church. Dennis Dickerson states that Payne "believed that the religiously untutored should be discouraged from making mischievous and unscriptural appeals to the Holy Ghost ... an exasperated Payne could do no more than ... denounce the excessive emotionalism and callisthenic gyrations of seemingly spirit-filled worshipers."[3] For this reason Payne concluded that revival methods were extravagant modes of worship and were more of a liability than an asset.[4]

It could be debated as to the degree, which A.M.E. clergy adhered to Payne's conservative pneumatological views; however, it is clear that the spirit of revival was vigorously embraced. During the height of the mid-nineteenth century, as revivals were sweeping the country, A.M.E. congregations were fully involved and eager participants in the spiritual outpouring. Bishop Benjamin Tanner writes in his memoir, *An Apology for African Methodism*,

> The Rev. John Cornish was appointed to the charge of Bethel Church, in June, 1857. The following winter he proposed a special effort in his Church for the revival of the work of God. By direction, he said, of the Holy Ghost, he called upon me to conduct that revival meeting; I accepted the appointment, and the result was that I never witnessed such a revival meeting before nor since that time. Not less than 400 souls were converted, 300 of whom joined Bethel, Church, Philadelphia.[5]

As African Methodism expanded its missionary efforts outside of North America, the tension between the revivalist religiosity of Richard Allen and the reserved sobriety of Daniel Payne would find new arenas in which the variance would progress. However, when the A.M.E. Church was organized in Jamaica, West Indies, revival techniques were vigorously welcomed and Allen's emotive worship style was enthusiastically embraced. It quickly became clear to early missionaries that organized the A.M.E.

---

3. Dickerson, *Reflections*, 52–53. Daniel Payne was charged with the task of creating a motto for the A.M.E. Church. He proposed, "God our Father, Christ Our Redeemer, Man Our Brother" at the 1856 General Conference. Dickerson argues that his deletion of the Holy Spirit reveals his suspicion of the ways in which the activity of the Holy Spirit would be expressed and interpreted by unlearned clergy and members of A.M.E. churches.

4. Dickerson, *Reflections*, 54.

5. Tanner, *Apology for African Methodism*, 170.

JAMAICA AND REVIVALISM

Church in Jamaica that most of the laity, and many of the clergy, joined because of the social egalitarianism of Allen's message, and the emotionalism of Allen's African Methodist worship; however, their socio-historical reality provided them with ideologies and praxis which did not completely align with the doctrine and discipline of the North American A.M.E. Church. A letter dated June 27, 1916, from Rev. G. J. Hollar to the Director of the A.M.E. Board of Missions states,

> I would also suggest to you to remove Rev's. Patterson and Bailey to some other field outside Jamaica so that they might *learn* the *workings* of the A.M.E. Church, and for goodness sake, send a good strong man as P.E. to build up the work in the island.[6]

The socio-cultural reality of religious Jamaica is vitally connected with revival, which contributes distinctive components to the popular Jamaican religiosity that will be discussed in the next section.

Jamaica's Revival Historical Narrative

The word "revival" cannot be used in reference to religious practices in Jamaica without understanding the socio-historical periods in which nineteenth-century revivals shaped the spirituality of masses of Jamaicans. There is a traceable historical point of departure in Jamaica, when religious revival occurrences became *Revivalism,* that is, a recognizable systematic religious belief and behavior among many Christian adherents. The spiritual roots of Revivalism are situated in the traditional religions of Central and West Africa. John Mbiti effectively argues that religion for African peoples is an ontological phenomenon, which answers the universal questions of existence. Traditional religion in Africa encompasses a complexity of ideologies and practices which necessarily generate a wide range of cultures. The precise ethnicity and demographic information of the hundreds of African tribes which were enslaved in Jamaica cannot be known to a high degree of certainty.[7] There is much contention among these scholars

---

6. Hollar, "Missionary Correspondence." "P. E." is short for "Presiding Elder," the supervisory and intermediate ministerial office within the A.M.E. Church, which supervises pastors within a specified district and reports to the presiding bishop. It is the writer's strong assumption that Hollar is referring to the presence of Revival Zion practices in the ministries of Patterson and Bailey as he recommends them for further education in the principles of the A.M.E. Church.

7. Various research studies on African slave demography have been published in

with regard to the specific number of Africans who were brought across the Atlantic as slaves. There is slightly more consensus on the geographical regions and tribal origins of persons who formed enslaved Jamaican society. Imprecise, incomplete, and unreliable records from shipping manifests, forts, and other corporate entities involved in the transatlantic slave trade compel leading authorities to offer tentative conclusions. Patterson's conclusions are most helpful for this project, as he extrapolates historical data which illustrates the proportion of Africans to whites and the relative size of different African ethnic groups in Jamaica, without descending into dizzying statistical detail.

Orlando Patterson argues that the tribal origins of enslaved persons in Jamaica almost all came from a 5,000-mile section of the African continent that stretches from Senegal down to Cape Negro. Furthermore, Patterson utilizes the six major trading centers on the west coast of Africa to ascertain the main tribal groups in the geographic region, those tribes most likely to become enslaved, and their contact with Europeans involved in the slave trade. These main areas of slave trade were Senegambia, Sierra Leone and the Windward Coast, the Gold Coast, the Slave Coast, the Bight of Benin and the region of the Niger and Cross deltas, and southwestern Africa from the Cameroons down to Cape Negro.[8] The peoples that populated this vast region belonged to several distinct linguistic families. Most of the enslaved Africans from these areas were: Kru speaking Mandingoes from Sierra Leone and the Windward Coast; the Akan speaking Ashanti or Koromantyns from the Gold Coast; Ewe speaking and Yoruba speaking from the Slave Coast; the Ibo from the Bight of Benin, and the Bantu peoples from Southwestern Africa or the Congo.

There is disagreement among scholars about the manner in which distinct African cultural traits predominate in different parts of the New World, i.e., Haiti with the Yoruba, Jamaica to the Ashanti, and so forth.[9]

LePage, *Jamaican Creole*; Patterson, *Sociology of Slavery*; Curtin, *Two Jamaicas*; Inikori, *Forced Migration*.

8. Patterson, *Sociology of Slavery*, 113–14.

9. Alleyne argues that demographic evidence suggests that African culture was able to survive because there was great cultural homogeneity among the enslaved groups brought to the New World and to Jamaica specifically. Sidney Mintz and Richard Price contrast Alleyne and Herskovits with an argument that recent studies suggest that slaves transported to New World colonies were more ethnically heterogeneous than previously believed. They posit that an African cultural heritage with strong continuities into any new colony must be defined abstractly, with a focus on values rather than sociocultural forms which buttress and shape behavior, and finally "with an examination of what

JAMAICA AND REVIVALISM

Pioneer anthropologist, Melville J. Herskovits is considered by most to be the Father of African Studies in the twentieth-century academy.[10] His 1941 masterpiece, *The Myth of the Negro Past*, details the significant, continued influence of African cultural elements in lives of African descendants throughout the diaspora. Herskovits presented several types of "Africanisms"—his vivid descriptions of retained behavior and beliefs—which implied the cultural assimilation of traditional African culture in the New World.[11] Herskovits's work has been thoroughly reconsidered and revised in the past half century by scholars who have created more nuanced views in light of the increased sensitivity and awareness of the social constructs regarding race and culture. E. Franklin Frazier was the first scholar to oppose Herskovits's position, claiming in his 1964 book, *The Negro Church in America*, that the trauma of the transatlantic slave trade and the inhumane conditions of enslavement eroded the essence of African cultural forms in the New World over time, except in isolated areas, such as the Carolina Sea Islands.[12] Others such as Winthrop Hudson, Sidney Mintz, and Richard Price also conclude that the socio-historical evidence of African cultural survivals is weak and that an overemphasis on African survivals diminish and distort the creative innovation of African descendants and black churches in the New World.

This author upholds the scholarship positions of Herskovits, Alleyn, Peter Paris, Jason Young, and others, which maintain that African religious continuities from the Mother continent can be discovered throughout the diaspora, and while expressed in diverse cultural forms, there is evidence of unity in the fundamental essence of African spirituality.[13] Despite the

---

George M. Foster labels 'cognitive orientations.'" See Mintz and Price, *Birth of African-American Culture*; Fulop and Raboteau, *African-American Religion*, 39–53.

10. A few contemporary scholars are revisiting the notion of Herskovitz's precedence, citing the importance of W. E. B. DuBois's work and other scholars during the Harlem Renaissance.

11. Herskovits, *Myth of the Negro Past*, 233–34. One of these retained Africanisms was the symbolic importance of water within Ashanti and Yoruba traditional religions and the ritual of immersion in the religious life of the Black Baptist church.

12. Frazier, *Negro Church in America*.

13. Mbiti, *African Religions and Philosophy*, 15–16. John Mbiti divides African religion/spirituality into five categories:
   a) GOD as ultimate explanation of genesis and sustenance of man and all things
   b) Spirits consist of extra-human beings and spirits of men who died a long time ago.
   c) Man, including human beings alive and about to be born
   d) Animals and plants, the remainder of biological life

fact that material support of their religious worldview was not transported to the New World, Africans brought their sacred cosmology with them, and this African worldview was re-integrated into a New World religious consciousness that survived and adapted in different forms under different conditions of enslavement and colonial subjugation. According to Patterson, the societal development on the island of Jamaica was distinctly altered by the large extent of absenteeism of a dominant white Jamaican community. Following the logic of this position, it is self-evident that strong continuities upholding an African religious worldview would be able to retain vitality in the absence of persons committed to its decline. Furthermore, the unintended consequence of absenteeism is highlighted in this project—by the fact that until very recently, A.M.E. bishops did not reside in the overseas episcopal districts. Therefore, the oversight of clerical training and the management of the churches by a presiding prelate was minimal at best. Patterson's argument exposes the problem of absent authority for societies and institutions.

The earliest writings by eighteenth- and nineteenth-century British observers, who travelled to Jamaica, depict the dominance of the Koromantyn or Ashanti culture in religion and language among the enslaved and Maroon Jamaican populous.[14] Mervyn Alleyne argues that the demographic evidence suggests that the Gold Coast was the main source of Jamaica bound Africans during the most important period of Jamaican societal formation, 1660–1700.[15] "The languages and culture (Akan culture) of this area are highly homogeneous—far more than other slave-trading areas. Dianne Stewart posits that the religiosity of Central African communities also had tremendous influence in the shaping of African Jamaican religiosity."[16] The African thought systems of the Kongo, Dahomean, Ga

---

e) *Phenomena and objects without biological life.*

14. Bryan Edwards published *History of the British Colonies in the West Indies* in 1793, R. C. Dallas published *History of the Maroons* in 1803, and W. J. Gardner published *A History of Jamaica* in 1873. All concur that Koromantyn was the most influential of all the other African ethnic groups in Jamaica. Koromantyn is spelled in numerous ways (i.e., Coromantyn, Koromanti, Coromantee) to describe the Akan speaking tribes from the Gold Coast.

15. Alleyne relies upon LePage and Patterson's usage of the records of English joint-stock companies which held a monopoly on the slave trade, all of whose headquarters were on the Gold Coast at this time. See Alleyne, *Africa*, 41.

16. Stewart, *Three Eyes for the Journey*, 64.

along with the Akan make important contributions to the religious cultural history of Jamaica.

Belief and Praxis in African-Jamaican Religiosity

My curiosity was piqued while observing/participating in a baptismal rite within a Jamaican A.M.E. Church that uniquely utilized symbols and imagery to infuse rich and complex religious meaning into the ritual. Contrary to the sobriety and routine manner in I had witnessed baptism performed within the North American A.M.E. Church that had shaped my ecclesial identity—this ritual was effervescent, lively and appeared to be transformative for all participants. The symbolism and imagery in the ritual of immersion mediated the manifestation of a new form of reality through the surviving elements of African traditional religion in the sociocultural milieu of Jamaica—as developed along the trajectories of belief and praxis. Scholars of West African traditional religions, such as Mervyn Alleyne, maintain that there is a remarkable uniformity in the supernatural beliefs of West African people.[17] Stewart states that continuities can also be observed among Central African religious patterns. The sociocultural evidence strongly suggests that there had to have been considerable cultural exchange among the enslaved Africans, such that an African-Jamaican religious consciousness with predominate Akan influence emerged by the end of the eighteenth century. This African-Jamaican religiosity, in its most conservative form, has been continuously practiced by the Maroon communities, who have maintained the strongest African retentions in language and religion through esoteric belief and praxis.[18] However, within popular Jamaican society, this African Jamaican religiosity later evolved through syncretism with Christianity.

Akan peoples believe in the existence of a Supreme Being. The Ultimate Deity has several names, *Onyankopon, Nyankupon, Odomankoma*, and *Nyame*. The religious world of the Asante in the West African country of Ghana begins with *Nyame*, the Unknowable One. There are no shrines

---

17. Geoffrey Parrinder's *West African Religions*, published in 1950, demonstrated remarkable symmetry in the belief systems and praxis among various tribes in West Africa.

18. Kenneth Bilby, a North American anthropologist, has conducted extensive research among Maroon communities in the Jamaican parishes of St. Elizabeth, Manchester, Portland, and St. Mary, has confirmed the continuities of Central and West African religious practices in the 1990s and early twenty-first century.

or priests to venerate this deity as God, yet this Divine presence pervades the Akan religious consciousness. A familiar myth relating to the origin of Akan culture explains the separation of humanity from the presence of God. In the myth, the heavens and the earth are very close together, and an old woman, known as *Aberewa*, is preparing *fufu*, the traditional meal among the Akan. *Fufu* requires the use of a mortar and pestle, to grind the tubers in order to make the paste. The noise of the banging of the mortar and pestle is so loud and powerful that it bangs against the heavens and causes God to move away. In Akan tradition, *Ananse*, the spider, is a prankster. He, like *Nyame*, has no shrines or priests, but his divinity is also pervasive and engulfs Asante culture. At the time of creation, *Ananse* was a companion to *Nyame*, rivaling him by creating negative and positive components of human existence.

> Ananse brought disease into the world in the following manner. In the process of bathing a sick girl, Ananse gathered all human diseases into a gourd. The girl recovered and grew into a beautiful woman, and Ananse married her. But he was obliged to give her to God, because he had once promised to find him a beautiful wife and had failed to do so. When God began to dance with the woman, Ananse struck her for spite with the gourd in which he had placed the diseases, and they all spilled out. This is how diseases, both fatal and non-fatal, entered into human society.[19]

There are a myriad of stories regarding the exploits of *Ananse*, which provide a means for the Asante to find meaning in the chaos that often interrupts human life in serendipitous ways.

There are lesser deities called *abosom*, who have derivative powers from *Nyame*, the Creator. These lesser gods inhabit trees, rivers, animals and plants, among other aspects of nature. Lastly, there are the spirits of the ancestors, who broaden the spiritual world and provide constant links between the world of the living and the world beyond the earthly realm. The Supreme Being is transcendent, distant from the human world, therefore little homage or attention is given. Instead, rituals are constructed to appease and honor the lesser deities and ancestral spirits, who have direct interrelation with the material world. Many of these spirits are prone to capriciousness, which can wreak havoc on an individual or community. It is the responsibility of the priest or priestess to maintain communion with intermediary deities and spirits to ensure the health and prosperity

---

19. Bilby, *True Born Maroons*, 15.

of the community, which is measured and monitored by the utilization of religious ritual, medicine, and witchcraft.

The Akan word for priest is *okomfo* (plural, *akomfo*). Persons become priests and priestesses in an elaborate initiation process whereby one gains the esoteric cultural knowledge of the spiritual world in which their people interrelate. This esoteric knowledge is gained within a pedagogical structure, which differentiates between the supernatural categories of ritual, medicine, and witchcraft. The role of the *okomfo* was a social one and the worship services were public affairs. In West Africa, medicine is anything, which possesses a power or is the dwelling place of a spiritual being.[20] This becomes vitally important for being able to distinguish between a good medicine man, who combines good medicine with ordinary herbs for beneficial purposes; and the bad medicine man, who is engaged in malicious activities which harm, hurt, and destroy others, even to the point of death. In Akan spirituality, healing is paramount and Asante religious leaders in traditional religious communities are often called upon to generate health and well-being among their members. The skills of herbalists, as well as incantations, are used along with familiar birds and animals that may be the embodiment of beneficial physical or spiritual aid.[21]

Witchcraft is essentially religious activity employed of antisocial magic. The Twi word for "witch" is *obayifo*. The name *bayi komfo* literally means, *priest of witchcraft*. The work of the *obayifo* is in opposition to that of the priest/priestess whose role enhances communal good. In fact, the two words used by early observers in Jamaica to describe African religious belief were *obeah* and *myalism*. Initially, *obeah* was used by early observers in a general sense to describe all supernatural beliefs and practices among the slaves, including *myalism*. Edward Long, the early Jamaican historian; uses the word in this manner.[22] *Obeah* is the art of sorcery, practiced in private, or in secret and reflects the destructive forces of a society under stress.

20. Malidoma Somé provides insight on the importance of his medicine as an African living in contemporary Western society: "When I travel to conferences, I always take my medicine bag with me. I have always been afraid to check it in the baggage for fear that it will somehow be lost—a terrible thought to contemplate since without it and the magical objects it contains, I would not be able to do the many . . . divinations I perform for people each year" (Somé, *Of Water and the Spirit*, 7).

21. Western scholars would often describe these beliefs and practices as *animism*—an ideology in which spirits occupy various living organisms and other phenomena. Mbiti was the first to offer a rebuttal on the grounds that God, spirits and divinities are a part of African traditional religion, just as they are in other world religions.

22. Long, *History of Jamaica*, 416. Long was the first to write about *obeah*, describing

By contrast, *myal* may be seen as a force of social integration, focused on the exposure of *obeah*, and defusing its power with communal values expressed in public ceremonies and ritual. The origin of the word for *myal* is unknown; however, it is often associated with a plant, the juice of which is used to induce trances. As priests within certain slave communities, *myal* men were herbalists who utilized the *myal* weed to produce a trance mimicking death, during a ceremony where drumming, singing, dancing and incantations occurred, and then another herbal preparation would be administered which would resurrect the new initiate into the *myal* society. Mervyn Alleyne states that the initiation ritual mimics characteristics of West African secret cult activity.[23] The atmosphere of mystery and secrecy would be utilized to resist the harshness of the new social context in which enslaved Africans found themselves. Therefore, this religious tradition was one in which a community of persons were connected through an ideology which promoted the advantages of membership as exemption from pain, sickness, and premature death, especially as the result of the inhumane conditions of living under the control of white slave owners. Following the lead of M. J. Field, Patterson places medicine and religion in separate existential categories within African cosmology. He describes the herbal use within *myalism* as a resemblance of West African good medicine, but admits that the dance ritual introduces elements of religion.[24] Later writers such as Baptist missionary James Phillipo, and Presbyterian minister, Hope Masterson Waddell record their observations of the *myal* dance as practiced within the indigenous African Jamaican religiosity of the 1840s.

> There we found them in full force and employment, forming a ring, around which were a multitude of onlookers. Inside the circle some females performed a mystic dance, sailing round and round, and wheeling in the centre with outspread arms, and wild looks and gestures. Others hummed, or whistled a low monotonous tone, to which the performers kept time, as did the people around also, by hands and feet and the swaying of their bodies. A man, who seemed to direct the performance, stood at one side, with folded arms, quietly watching their evolutions.[25]

---

obeah men as conjurers and magicians.

23. Alleyne, *Africa*, 85.
24. Alleyne, *Africa*, 188.
25. Waddell, *Twenty-Nine Years in West Indies*, 189.

JAMAICA AND REVIVALISM

Scholars such as Alleyne and E. Kamau Braithwaite agree that *myalism* came to be the dominant form of religion that developed among the slaves in Jamaica and that it was the first religious organization of Africans in Jamaica. Waddell's account hints of smug ethnocentrism, however provides details that are necessary for understanding the purpose of the *myal* dance. He described a dance by persons in the form of a ring, makes a distinction between the ring dancers and others, and notes the direction by a leader—all elements which subsequent observers assent to and which would be borne out in the later version of Jamaican Revival religion. The ceremony was designed in large part to exhibit the spiritual ability of the religious leader.

Early African Jamaican spirituality consisted of a metaphysical anthropology, which provided the philosophical framework for the functions of both *obeah* and *myalism* within slave society. Firstly, humanity possessed a spirit which departed upon death. This spirit was believed to return to the ancestral land and dwell among the other ancestral spirits. However, before the spirit embarked upon the journey, it hovered over the spot of death or burial—promoting a culture of elaborate burial rituals designed to appease the spirit and facilitate a pleasurable environment for its travel. Later, the ancestral homeland gradually would lose prominence in the consciousness of the enslaved Jamaicans and the precaution would shift to simply placating the spirits of friends and relatives and the neutralization of those of one's enemies. These spirits were known as *duppies,* a term which survives in Jamaica implying spirits which roam after death. Another spirit, called the *shadow,* belonged to living people; this concept is of special interest because it was by the capturing or nailing of this element that *obeah* men and women harmed their victims and, by its release, *myal* men healed their adherents. *Myal* men were often present at funerals to catch shadows and make sure that they were properly buried with the body to protect the community from its malignant properties. Terms and concepts consonant with metaphysical dimensions of a human being's personality such as *duppy, shadow, spirit,* and *soul* are often riddled with ambiguity when defined by scholars or within popular Jamaican understanding. Patterson claims that the Ga tribe of Ghana, believes that *susuma* means the essence of human personality and that the *shadow,* a loosely defined *kla* concept, is related to the *susuma,* so when the *kla* departs, the victim dies.[26] Roger Bastide speaks of similar popular religious beliefs among religious com-

---

26. Patterson, *Sociology of Slavery,* 189.

munities in Suriname. He points to two souls, the *akra*, related to the Twi word, *kra*, meaning "soul," which is born and dies within the individual and provides protection from evil forces; alongside the *yorka*, which leaves the body at death and wanders about.[27] Religious historian Albert Raboteau states, while analyzing the early slaves concepts of reincarnation and return to Africa upon death, that there are several components to the traditional African idea of the soul.[28]

The retention of African spirituality within the popular Jamaican religiosity that would inform the African Methodist Episcopal Church in Jamaica would be most vividly frequently observed in burial rites. Even today, members of the Jamaican A.M.E. Church are among the few remaining communities of faith that frequently honor their dead with the nine-night ceremony.[29] The observance is traditionally commemorated by clergy, church family, friends and kin holding numerous wakes and making nine nightly pilgrimages to the *'dead yard'*—meaning, the colloquial term for the home where the recently deceased lived. On the ninth night there is a big celebration with a large crowd—all are welcome to attend, eat, drink, sing and dance until the wee hours of morning.[30] The funeral takes place the morning after the 'ninth night' of celebration. Edna G. Bay investigates the implications of the use of *collective memory* to approach the question of the meaning of the Atlantic slave-trade for Africans who remained in Africa.[31] She utilizes collective memory's link to presently existent group identities, psychoanalytic and trauma theory to ascertain the manner in which the emotional damage of the slave trade was expressed by the descendants of

---

27. Bastide, *African Civilizations*, 100.

28. Raboteau, *Slave Religion*, 32.

29. Churches and clergy that serve the upper and middle class sector of Jamaicans have historically discouraged the practice of the nine-night ceremony because of its association with African spirituality and heathenish ignorance. As a result, the burial ritual is often scorned and ridiculed by middle-upper class Jamaicans, and/or those who have assimilated their socio-cultural religious values.

30. Although the descriptions are dated and no longer accurate and applicable to current nine night practices in the Jamaican A.M.E. church; an early scholarly contribution of the nine night funerary ritual was written by noted anthropologist George Eaton Simpson. See Simpson, "Nine Night Ceremony in Jamaica," 329–35. My father's side of the family did not typically participate in the nine night because prior to my father's conversion to African Methodism, they were 'respectable' Catholics during the mid-twentieth century. However, when my beloved Aunt Maysie passed in 2017, my cousin's husband persuaded the family to honor her life with the traditional ritual.

31. Bay and Mann, *Rethinking the African Diaspora*, 48.

the survivors. She argues that the scale of the long term emotional damage can be identified and studied within the ritual practices of living cultures. "Collective memory works from signs of the past in the present: our empathy for what we know of the past, our sense of who we are and where we come from, and our study of rituals, symbols, and actions that could plausibly be linked to a former social or political condition."[32] This argument for collective memory as expressed in Jamaican popular religiosity through its burial ritual could be extended to the argument for the retention of African spirituality in the baptismal rituals of the early A.M.E. Church of Jamaica.

African spirituality framed the relationships which existed among the enslaved persons. Social harmony was conducted among enslaved persons through the check and balance system between the communal spiritual work of the *myal*-man (*okomfo*), and the private sorcery of the *obeah*-man (*obayifo*). Patterson describes *myalism* and *obeah* within slave society as being employed to prevent, detect, and punish crime. All sorts of ingredients were used as fetishes by *obeah* men to perform their work, however, early reports state that a favorite item used to detect crime was grave dirt—anyone suspected of a crime would be forced to assemble at a grave, ingest it, upon which the guilty party's intestine was expected to swell and burst.[33] The *obeah*-man was adept at the secret art of poisoning, while the *myal*-man was a skilled herbalist.

This dichotomy breaks down slightly when one considers the function of *obeah* and *myal* in the relationships between the enslaved and the planter class. Because *obeah* played such a large part in the numerous rebellions of the slaves, the planter class developed an early disdain and fear toward slave religious practices. On the plantations where *obeah* men were enslaved, the slave owners were constantly afraid of being poisoned and marked for death via *obeah* practices. This resulted in early legislation which outlawed public rituals to occur in many territories throughout the Caribbean. Acts passed in 1696 prevented the assembly of large groups of slaves on Sundays and holidays.[34] This ban forced the *okomfo* to perform his work as clandestinely as the *obayifo* might. The most renowned legislation with clear language against the practice of *obeah* was the Jamaica *Code Noir*, passed after the rebellion of 1760. "Negroes found with blood, feathers, parrots beaks, dog's

---

32. Bay and Mann, *Rethinking the African Diaspora*, 49.
33. Patterson, *Sociology*, 191, citing Leslie, *New History of Jamaica*, 308.
34. *Acts of the Assembly from 1681 to 1737*, 55.

teeth, alligator's teeth, broken bottles, grave dirt, rum, egg shells . . . will be declared guilty of Obeah."[35]

During the formative years of Jamaican slave society, African spirituality was being constantly reinforced by new arrivals of slaves from Africa, therefore the integrity of African religious belief was maintained, and several documents report that the most knowledgeable practitioners of slave religion were African-born.[36] These African born religious leaders would have been pressed to perform rites to harm the slave owners by their adherents. It is difficult to ascertain among the numerous attempts to poison planters and organize rebellions whether the culprit was a captured priest, *okomfo,* or witchdoctor, *obayifo.* Violent resistance to the plantocracy was led by men who were revered as persons with a heightened spiritual awareness throughout the Americas. Among these were Cuffy, the leader of a revolt in Guyana in 1763, Tacky, the man who inspired the 1760 rebellion in Jamaica, and Boukman, the religious leader of the St. Domingue slave revolt in 1790. The difficulty of teasing out the activity of the "bad" religious leader versus the "good" religious leader becomes apparent as one reads the surviving documents from biased white observers of early Jamaican society, who cast all religious activity under the evil cast of *obeah*.[37] Alleyne argues that due to the harsh conditions under which slaves lived and the ban on their holding public religious gatherings, likely combined to make *obeah* more important than other components in the enslaved community's religion. Dale Bisnauth argues against this position, he claims that in fact, most of the religious leaders were *akomfo* who functioned in the slave communities' best interest, hence were relied upon to use "good" spiritual ability to call upon the spirits to assist the enslaved in their acts of resistance. "The Caribbean *obayifo*, on the other hand, wrought harm to slaves on behalf of clients for fees; or . . . to avenge himself on those who crossed him."[38] Joseph Williams made a distinction in his discussion of the roles between the work of *obeah* men and *myal* men, labeled the *myal* men as the ones who,

> administered the terrible fetish oath mixing gunpowder with the rum and added grave dirt and human blood to the concoction that

---

35. *Acts of the Assembly from 1770 to 1783,* 256.

36. Edwards, *History, Civil and Commercial, in West Indies,* 2:xix.

37. Bryan Edwards and Edward Long provide the earliest accounts of African Jamaican religiosity in the eighteenth century; however, the two observations are flawed by ethnocentrism and cultural ignorance of the African cosmological worldview.

38. Bisnauth, *History of Religions in Caribbean,* 90.

was to seal upon the conspirators' lips the awful nature of the plot for liberty, steel their hearts to the dangerous undertaking. It was he who devised the mystic powder that was to make their bodies invulnerable and enable them to meet the white man's bullets.[39]

Unlike the Western world, within African cosmology good and evil are not definite opposites, and the moral complexity of Jamaica's slave society amplified this ambiguity. Dianne Stewart provides a vivid contrast to the prevailing definition of *obeah*; she argues that, "in the African Jamaican imagination, Obeah is capacity and encompasses unlimited operative meanings. It is the capacity to use energy dynamically, which requires specialized knowledge acquired naturally or through training."[40] Therefore the dichotomy that Western philosophy imposes between the two African religious traditions, *myal* and *obeah* is false and unsustainable—this work concurs with Stewart that moral neutrality is the best ideology to deal with the metaphysics and ethical dilemmas that shaped the religious practitioners of both traditions.[41] However, the encounter with Christianity would influence one tradition more than the other, the communal nature of *myalism* rendered it most likely to experience cultural contact and thus open to syncretism with Christian symbolism, doctrine, and ritual. *Myal* leaders and adherents who became converted, discovered that they were able to conduct public religious ceremony with little restriction, when they claimed the authority of Jesus Christ for their activities.

Missionary Contact

The importance of the church's role in the dismantling of oppression and evil in the lives of enslaved persons became most apparent through the work of missionaries to the island of Jamaica during the pre-emancipation era. The Wesleyan Methodists and the Baptists were most readily identified as supporters of abolition, while the Moravians who were the first missionaries to arrive were viewed as neutral upholders of the status quo. The African Methodist missionaries who arrived to Jamaica in the twentieth century would use the story of Richard Allen as social protest against the tentacles of Western colonial power that created racial disparity and

---

39. Williams, *Voodoos and Obeahs*, 146.
40. Stewart, *Three Eyes for the Journey*, 41.
41. Stewart, *Three Eyes for the Journey*, 11.

constantly threatened the economic and political stability of the island. In actuality, the imperial power of the metropolitan centers of modern Western culture provided the sufficient material and personnel resources to support successful missionary ventures. A religious phenomenon called the *cargo cult*, describes cultural contact in which the substitution of Western cultural forms destroys the native ceremonies of an indigenous people.[42] The cargo cult occurs at a point of cultural contact as a specific religious phenomenon with its own beliefs, practices, and corresponding visions and spirit possession.[43] The ritual of believer's baptism in popular Jamaican religiosity as inherited from the Native Baptist tradition could be viewed as a cultural religious dynamic of a cargo cult which continues to exhibit symbolic continuities in the African Methodist Episcopal Churches of Jamaica.

Christianity had been briefly introduced to Jamaica when the Roman Catholic Church arrived to the Caribbean during the invasion of the first Spanish conquistadors in the fifteenth century. Christobal Colón arrived on the island of Jamaica, then called *Xaymaca* by the indigenous people of the region, May 5, 1494. At the time the Spaniards were preoccupied with gold, a metal which Jamaica lacked, therefore Spain failed to invest significant resources in the colony. The number of Africans transported to Jamaica was much less than the other Spanish colonies of Cuba and South America, where gold could be mined. The period of Spanish colonization in Jamaica (1498–1655), required very little slave labor, and, although Spanish codes of the seventeenth century prescribed baptism for slaves within a year of the slaves' arrival from Africa, the evangelization process for enslaved persons by the Roman Catholic Church was typically cursory and insignificant.[44]

Jamaica was captured from Spain in 1655 by Oliver Cromwell, after his unsuccessful attempt to seize Santo Domingo, a prized and heavily fortified Spanish colony. The initial years of British rule were filled with frequent military skirmishes with the remnants of the Spanish Armada, until

---

42. The publication of *The Vailala Madness and the Destruction of Native Ceremonies in the Gulf District* by F.E. Willliams in 1923 spawned the scholarship on the phenomena of cargo cults.

43 Charles Long, the historian of religion, interprets the cargo cult as a religious phenomenon that describes the situation of cultural contact from the perspective of those subjugated during the conquest. He emphasizes the reappropriation of language and symbols of the colonizer by the colonized cult leader, for the purpose of creating a new form of humanity. See Long, *Significations*, 125–38.

44. Dale Bisnauth and Orlando Patterson are among the majority of scholars of the region which concur on this historical development.

JAMAICA AND REVIVALISM

1661, when Britain secured decisive control of the island. In 1661, martial law was discontinued and civil government was established, at which time the first resident Anglican clerics arrived as representatives of the Church of England.[45] Orlando Patterson states that the history of the Church of England on the island of Jamaica is perhaps one of the denomination's most disgraceful episodes in its history. The clergymen assigned to the island were frequently described by their contemporaries as being ill equipped and immoral. Edward Long declared that some were "better qualified to be retailers of salt-fish, or boatswain privateers than ministers of the gospel." Anglican Bishop Lynch lamented in 1671 that, "the condition of the Church be so low and the number of ministers be so few that they are not worth taking notice of." In 1740 C. Leslie gave "a dismal account" of the Church Affairs of the Island, declaring that the clergy "of a character so vile" as to be unmentionable and concluded that "they are generally the most finished of our Debauchers.'"[46] Their personal irreligiosity and complete neglect of evangelism contributed to the reputation of white Jamaican society as indifferent in religious matters, crude, corrupt, and decadent.

Throughout the Caribbean, the Church of England functioned in a distinctly different Erastian manner than the Mother church. The Caribbean State Church was deeply indebted to the power of sugar planters and governmental officials who composed the membership of the House of Assembly which voted on the terms of their clerical salary. The Governor assigned curates to pulpits and the clerics served at his pleasure. Most importantly, at the regional parish level, the planters composed the *vestry*—which functioned as a civil, as well as an ecclesiastical, body with the power to dictate the policy and program of the local parish church. Therefore, as members of the white ruling class, with few exceptions, Anglican clergymen shared the same proslavery ideological perspectives as the plantocracy. This ideology regarded enslaved Africans as treacherous barbarians without souls, who lacked the intellectual capacity to reason, and thus failed to see the value in Christianizing them. A neglected slave code of 1696 stipulated that slave owners should attempt to facilitate the

---

45. Bisnauth, *History of Religions*, 51, 52. Bisnauth reports that there were seven Anglican ministers of religion who served as naval and military chaplains during the military expedition which captured the island. However, the church was not established on the island until civil government was started. However, the Church of England was established after the dissolution of the Commonwealth occurred, therefore it was the church of the Restoration.

46. Patterson, *Sociology of Slavery*, 40.

conversion of the slaves and prepare them for baptism; however, the House of Assembly placed a prohibitive fee on for the cost of a baptism performed by the Church of England.

The first attempt to convert the enslaved community in Jamaica was begun by the Moravians in 1754. The evangelistic venture was small and was sponsored by Moravian members of the plantocracy, so their motives did not raise the apprehensions of the authorities. Three United Brethren or Moravian missionaries arrived to instruct and convert the slaves of the estates of two absentee proprietors in the parishes of St. Elizabeth and Westmoreland. The Moravians were to be settled on three estates and given land and resources in exchange for their oversight. Among their resources were slaves to provide domestic help and work the fields. The manner in which these Moravian ministers instructed the enslaved Africans appeased white society; they managed to retain societal support even when other missionaries suffered great persecution by the plantocracy in the violence-ridden years prior to emancipation. However, this support was garnered at the price of low response on the part of the slaves, who were reluctant to accept the gospel from pastors who were themselves, slave owners.[47]

Just the opposite was the case for the Baptists, who arrived on the island in 1782, in the person of George Liele, a formerly enslaved African who was among the first black(s not the first) ordained Baptist ministers in America. Liele was among the first generation of blacks who became converted during the First Great Awakening in colonial North America. The Methodist Revival in England provided a direct link to the conversion of enslaved Africans through the itinerant preaching of George Whitefield during the 1740s in Middle Colonies. The egalitarian nature of the revival brought various communions of faith together to emphasize the importance of the new birth, while diminishing doctrinal differences that were determined to be inconsequential to salvation. A journal entry of Whitefield on August 22, 1741, provides an example of his response to the unkind treatment that he received from Anglican clergymen in Charleston, South Carolina:

> Finding when I was here last, that Jesus Christ was not preached in the church, my conscience would not suffer me to attend on those

---

47. See Buchner, *Moravians in Jamaica*. Compared to the evangelistic program of the Dissenter missionaries who arrived after the Moravians, their successes dwarfed the United Brethren's venture. The number of slave converts and members was less than a thousand in 1838, nearly one hundred years after they began the work.

that preached there anymore. I therefore went to the Baptist and Independent meeting houses, where Jesus Christ was preached. I have administered the Sacrament thrice in a private house. Never did I see anything more solemn. The room was large, and most were in tears, as though they were weeping at their Saviour's Cross. ... I prayed for them all, and I hope the Lord will clothe them with the wedding garment. What was best, Baptists, Church folks, and Presbyterians, all joined together, and received according to the Church of England, except two, who desired to have it sitting: I willing complied, knowing that it was a thing quite indifferent.[48]

Whitefield's influence directly impacted several ministers who were to become leaders in the North American revival that occurred in New England and in the Middle Colonies. For example, Shubal Stearns, the leader of the Separatist Baptist revival, which began in North Carolina in 1755, became converted after hearing Whitefield preach in Massachusetts during the 1740s. Separatist Baptists like Stearns were not only known for the emotionalism of their worship, but also for an elevated sense of sacramentalism noted by their frequent observance of Holy Communion. From 1755 to 1765, Stearns and his team of exhorters and preachers spread the revival throughout North Carolina, as well as into southwestern Virginia and upstate South Carolina. Furthermore, it was the Separate Baptists who willingly accepted blacks as members into mixed churches and did not forbid or constrain the claims of dreams, visions, and trances during the black Baptist conversion process.

Separate Baptist revivalist leaders provided support for the first all-black Baptist congregations in North America. George Liele became converted in 1773 under the preaching of a white Separatist Baptist preacher named Rev. Matthew Moore, and soon Liele's owner, Henry Sharpe, who was a Baptist deacon, recognized his ministerial gifts and granted him his permission to travel. Once he obtained a license to preach, Liele began to conduct ministry fulltime; he traveled up and down the Savannah River, preaching on surrounding plantations wherever the slave owners permitted. He organized the first black independent Baptist congregation in Yama Craw near Savannah, Georgia, in 1777, and was among those who preached at the first organized black Baptist congregation in the Americas at Silver Bluff, South Carolina.[49] After the defeat of the British by Americans was

48. Whitefield, *George Whitefield's Journals*, 174.

49. The Rev. Waitstill Palmer was another white Separatist Baptist minister who had been influenced by George Whitefield; he baptized Shubal Stearn and also preached

imminent, Liele feared becoming reenslaved by the children of his former owner, therefore, he departed Georgia when the British Loyalists evacuated Savannah, Georgia, on July 20, 1782. He secured the passage for himself and his family by indebting himself to a Col. Kirkland, a British officer who had been reassigned to Jamaica. Liele left America as an indentured servant with his wife and four children, and after he repaid the Colonel, he began to preach to the enslaved Africans in Jamaica. His emotional preaching style appealed to the enslaved communities in Kingston and his congregation grew rapidly. A letter written by Liele, dated December 18, 1791, to Dr. Rippon of the British Baptist Missionary Society, shares autobiographical details along with ministry highlights.

> As soon as I had settled Col. Kirkland's demands on me, I had a certificate of my freedom from the vestry and governor, according to the act of this Island, both for myself and family. Governor Campbell left the Island. I began, about September 1784, to preach in Kingston, in a small private house, to a good smart congregation, and I formed the church with four brethren from America besides myself, and the preaching took very good effect with the poorer sort, especially the slaves.[50]

This was first among several letters that Liele wrote to the British Baptist Missionary Society to solicit support for his missionary work in Jamaica. This particular letter requested financial support to complete the construction on his first church. Liele's congregation that started with just four people in 1784 grew rapidly and he planned to build a church on three acres of his personal land in 1789. Liele's appeal was supported by a letter written to Dr. Rippon by Mr. Stephen Cooke, a member of the House of Assembly. Liele had gained the confidence of many influential members of Jamaican society during his period of indentureship to Col. Kirkland. The Baptist Missionary Society responded favorably to Liele's request; however, the funds that they sent were not enough to retire the debt owed and Liele

---

frequently to the black congregation at Silver Bluff. The Silver Bluff church was located on the plantation of a Mr. George Galphin, which was in close proximity to the plantations of Hugh and Jonathan Bryan; evangelical slave owners who had hosted The Rev'd John Wesley during his sojourn to the American colonies. Moreover, the Bryans were intimate acquaintances of George Whitefield. Therefore it is highly likely that George Liele learned the Methodist class leader system during his early years of itinerancy along the Savannah River as he preached for slave owners who encouraged the catechesis of their slaves, among which the Bryans would have been very prominent.

50. Liele et al., "Letters Showing the Rise and Progress," 71.

JAMAICA AND REVIVALISM

was thrown into debtors' prison. Liele was jailed twice for debt and once for insurrection. Three additional men from America would be most helpful to Liele in the early development of Baptist Church of Jamaica, especially while Liele was imprisoned. Moses Baker, George Lewis, and George Gibb are listed in the pantheon of Jamaica's pioneer Baptist preachers. Each of these men supported Liele's ministry and all provided four decades of consistent ministry in Jamaica, preaching, teaching, and baptizing in thriving congregations in and well beyond the first mission in Kingston. Liele's work expanded from St. Thomas to the east and westward into Spanish Town and St. Catherine, however his assistants proselytized across the island. Mechal Sobel states that black Baptist preachers such as Liele and his assistants, who were socialized within colonial North America, were the architects of a 'black Baptist Sacred Cosmos,' "While they saw themselves as fully Christian and did not recognize the African qualities in their world view, their new cosmos had enormous appeal and particular strength just because it was an Afro-Baptist cosmos."[51] In *Plantation Church*, Noel Erskine pivots away from Sobel's argument that Liele did not recognize Africa by stating that while Liele did not begin an African Church in Kingston, He does name the church, the Ethiopian Baptist Church.

> There was an early attempt by Liele to combine the question, "Where do we stand in relation to Jesus?" with the African question, "Where do we stand in relation to Africa?" This approach not only sought to merge issues of enculturation and acculturation, the search for survival with that of liberation, but it meant that the church combined questions of salvation and social justice. It is clear that Liele began a new tradition in Jamaica.[52]

The legacy of this cosmic worldview and/or new tradition would inform the fundamental understanding of baptism within the early African Methodist Episcopal Church in Jamaica.

Spirit Christians

Uniting African and Baptist elements into a new cohesive force, as defined by Sobel, forged this Afro-Baptist cosmos. While Liele and his other African American Baptist ministers may not have recognized the African

---

51. Sobel, *Trabelin' On*, 107.
52. Erskine, *Plantation Church*, 177.

elements in their faith, many enslaved African Jamaicans most certainly did and eagerly emphasized them as new converts to Christianity. African religiosity was allowed to flourish in Jamaica in ways that it could not in North America. Patterson's theory of absenteeism of leadership in white society is most useful for conceptualizing the social context in which the early enslaved Jamaicans converted to Christianity. He uses data derived from abstracts of wills relating to Jamaican estates during 1625–1792, the contents of which in almost every case went to relatives in England. "One can easily imagine that these inheritors, having no intimate link with the island . . . would gladly settle for an attorney in the island to supervise his or her estate, thus adding to the number of absentee owners."[53] The consequence of absentee ownership was magnified in a society in which the population disparity was so great between the dominant slave owner class and the enslaved.[54]

The lack of interest and oversight of the enslaved African religious practices by the dominant white society meant that Christianity could make no real impact on the African religious worldview until the last three or four decades of slavery. The manner in which Liele organized his Baptist converts unintentionally provided a vehicle in which African Jamaican religiosity was maintained and transmitted. In North America, Liele became acquainted with the class leader system, a Methodist innovation, and implemented it in Jamaica to organize his burgeoning membership. The system was easily adapted on Jamaican estates, where class leaders became known as daddies and mammies who held weekly meetings with enslaved converts, prepared candidates for baptism, and monitored the moral conduct of the members.

Although Liele and the other African American preachers were literate, many of the class leaders and most of the members were illiterate; therefore, conversion was a profound spiritual experience rather than a doctrinal or biblical revelation. The convert who desired baptism was expected to engage in serious contemplation and give evidence of his readiness to become a full member of the church. This requirement often took the form of relaying a particular dream or vision in which the convert saw her or himself in the presence of John the Baptist or Jesus Christ. The significance of dreams

53. Patterson, *Sociology*, 36.
54. For example, in 1788, the Jamaica census records that there were 1,314 whites to 226,432 slaves. In 1825, there were 25,000 whites, 30,000 free coloreds, 10,000 free blacks, and 340,000 slaves.

JAMAICA AND REVIVALISM

was widely accepted by African slaves and, as mentioned previously, was already a fundamental element of the Afro-Baptist cosmos introduced by Liele. As a pioneer pastor, Liele made every attempt to maintain an orthodox congregation in doctrine and in practice. In fact, the members of the central Kingston Chapel did reflect the social respectability of Eurocentric religiosity due to his active oversight. However, Liele and his assistants would gradually discover that many class leaders were incorporating unacceptable elements of African religiosity during their weekly gatherings. Many of these leaders became *de facto* spiritual guides, assuming a spiritual leadership role that resembled the *myal*-man or *myal* women. One of the deacons that Liele appointed to oversee his initial Kingston congregation was Thomas Nicholas Swigle.[55] "He was one of the first Creoles in Jamaica to be identified with the Afro-Jamaican Baptist church movement. He convinced a number of the members to withdraw from . . . [Liele] to organize another church."[56]

Therefore, almost from the beginning, especially in the rural areas of Jamaica, the members of the Baptist churches blended their new Christian beliefs with the old African beliefs. This was seen frequently in the public burial rites as baptized members continued to: hold wakes for several days to ensure the peaceful transition of the departed soul; arrange dramatic processions with the coffin; drum, dance, chant and chase shadows to capture unfriendly spirits which might linger to torment the living. In 1788, Liele sent Moses Baker to evangelize the enslaved persons on the plantations in the western area of Jamaica. The Moravian mission to St. Elizabeth had since severely declined, having been set up three decades prior to his arrival, and as the first black preacher to evangelize enslaved persons in that region, he discovered persons who had never been introduced to Christianity. Clement Gayle writes that following Baker's relocation, after two weeks of preaching and teaching, he had achieved a small degree of success, prompting one of the leading men to tell him,

55. The first notable split from Liele's church was with Thomas Swigle, a Jamaican colored man who had been ordained Deacon by Liele. After discussing the lawsuit between Liele and Swigle, which Swigle won; Clement Gayle hints that Swigle may have allowed more unorthodox spirit phenomena to occur within in his church, such as trances and speaking in tongues, practices which Liele strongly discouraged. Gayle writes, "Possibly because Swigle was a son of the soil, he had advantages over Liele." Knowing the importance of spirit possession in the African Jamaican religious cosmology would have provided a significant advantage for Swigle, who is historically characterized as the first Jamaican Baptist preacher to incorporate African Jamaican religiosity within his church.

56. Pugh, *Pioneer Preachers in Paradise*, 34.

REBAPTISM CALMLY CONSIDERED

[he] agreed that what he was saying was good, but the life of the negroes was such that that they could not follow it. In order to make his point he took Baker first to his own house and showed him bottles, horns, and other things employed in the working of witchcraft. He then informed Baker that similar things could be found at the homes of other negroes.[57]

This letter from Moses Baker describes the prevalent usage of fetishes in the religious expression among the enslaved community. Baker's letter further indicates that the fetish use is witchcraft, and thus antithetical to Christianity, as the North American Afro Baptist cosmos did not accommodate fetishism. In spite of this obstacle, Baker was able to convert many enslaved Africans to Christianity and soon organized several churches on many plantations in the northwest region of the island. It soon became apparent that the converts were unable or unwilling to completely relinquish many of their African religious practices. The Afro Baptist cosmos readily absorbed elements of both *obeah* and *myalism* within Native Baptist culture. Barry Chevannes argues that the foundational religious structure of the Native Baptist movement is *Myal*.[58] In 1812, Liele and Baker realized the ministry was losing ground to Myalism and they wrote an urgent letter to the British Baptist Missionary Society (BMS) appealing for missionaries willing to preach and teach in the Jamaican mission field. The BMS responded favorably, but slowly; the first English missionary would not arrive until 1814.

The first BMS missionary was a Mr. John Rowe, a young man who had studied at Bristol Academy in Bristol, England, and was a member of the Baptist Church at Yeovil, in Somersetshire. The written instructions given by Dr. Rippon, illustrate to Rowe that he would be coming to an established mission field with thirty decades of development, as evidenced by its organization, numbers of churches throughout the island, and membership of 8,000 persons.

---

57. Gayle, *George Liele*, 29–32. Moses Baker arrived to Jamaica from New York in 1782, he subsequently met George Liele and was baptized. Next to Liele, the name of Moses Baker ranks the highest among the pioneers of the Baptist Church in Jamaica.

58. The religious structure was predominately *myal*; however, the most predominate *obeah* element was that of the ritual of taking an oath or vow. The vows or oath taking continues to be an influential element within popular Jamaican religiosity. The baptismal vow in the immersion ritual is where the early A.M.E. Church of Jamaica would fully employ it. See Stewart, *Three Eyes for the Journey*, 129.

JAMAICA AND REVIVALISM

> You are going to unite with an aged man, in the work of instructing negroes, a man whose character been able to obtain, as well as his years, him inferior to you in knowledge, but never make him feel himself to be so, and in those things wherein his age and experience will naturally give him the precedency, you will, we trust, as naturally yield it. between you, and if he be more tenacious of some peculiarities than Let there be no strife necessary, yet if they are not evil, for love's sake bear with them.[59]

Rowe and the other English Baptist missionaries that soon would follow him to Jamaica were direct inheritors of the religious flame that George Whitefield and John Wesley sparked in England's countryside and the North American colonies during the eighteenth century. The age of revival, which challenged the Anglican churches complacency in England and in North America, invited the masses to hear the gospel of the new birth and to become converted to God in a new brand of emotional Christianity by becoming overwhelmed by the power of the Holy Spirit. In less than fifteen years after Rowe arrived to Jamaica, both Liele and Baker had died, and by 1831, the BMS missionaries had taken over the leadership of most Baptist churches throughout Jamaica. Mission church leadership passed from black to white, a phenomenon that endured for more than 140 years. Nevertheless, black Baptist churches with black leaders who combined Christianity with African religiosity maintained a strong presence, as many slaves preferred the syncretism of Christianity with the influence and power of African religious belief and praxis. These churches would become identified as Native Baptist churches—independent black churches with black religious leaders. By the 1820s this Myal-Christianity syncretism was thoroughly integrated into the indigenous culture of the majority of African Jamaican Christian population. Nineteenth-century Presbyterian missionary, Hope Waddell reflects on this dilemma:

> The way was prepared for Baptist missionaries by people of the same name from America. . . . George Liele, a black man from Savannah, Georgia founded that peculiar body since known as the Native Baptists. His successors, Gibb, Clarke and Moses Baker and others extended his system. . . . Moses Baker settled in St. James's parish . . . [he] appointed leaders over classes among the negro houses of many estates. He seems to have been a good man . . . but ill-informed and most superstitious. He could do little in giving sound instruction in all the classes he had formed, being able to

---

59. Gayle, *George Liele*, 30, 32.

visit them only at night, and having no regular Sabbath or church services, ... initiated them in a strange system of truth and error, which his leaders carried to the length of a monstrous superstition ... disorders so greatly multiplied which he could no longer rectify, that he applied for an English Baptist missionary to succeed him in his congregation.... The grand doctrine of these people was the Spirit's teaching. It gave life. The written word was a dead letter. If they could not read the Bible they could do without it.... The Spirit was sought in dreams and visions of the night, which thus became the source of their spiritual life.... The connection of these people with the English missionaries ... promised to be beneficial ... but proved ... to be a permanent injury.[60]

Waddell's reflection teases out a significant distinction between the European missionaries and the Native Baptists, the lack of emphasis on the written word of God. While literacy was valued and appreciated by Native Baptists—they were fundamentally Spirit Christians who understood that knowledge acquired through spiritual experience was a credible and *preferred* epistemological source. The African religious worldview coveted spiritual consciousness, by which Spirit Christians acquired potent intuition through intentional engagement with the invisible world filled with spirits and ancestral spirits. Spirit Christians understood the importance of literacy for navigating the visible world controlled by dominant white society. However, African cosmology sustained them with an epistemology, which the missionaries could not comprehend, one that accentuated the complexity of the unseen world of the spirit and the vital importance of creating and maintaining right relationship with its inhabitants. Popular Jamaican religiosity highly regards the ability to perceive and negotiate the complexity of the spirit realm.

Jamaica's Post-Emancipation Myal Revival

Notwithstanding their epistemological disconnect, the missionaries made their most productive gains in the years prior to and just after emancipation. The missionaries were the only group of Europeans who provided sustainable measures of educational and spiritual reform among the enslaved population. Due to their interest, all churches grew rapidly for a decade after emancipation, then began to decline in the late 1840s, as

---

60. Waddell, *Twenty Nine Years*, 25–26.

social tensions began to emerge in the post emancipation climate. Philip Curtin reports that the Baptist membership increased from 10,000 in 1831 to 34,000 by 1845. "All the missionary churches gained members till about 1845 and then lost from a quarter to a half of those members between 1845 and 1865, and the movement of loss and gain had secular as well as religious causes."[61] The collapse of sugar production in St. Domingue during the late eighteenth century had ushered in a period of great prosperity to the British West Indian sugar planter, but economic misfortune was looming. The abolition of the slave trade in 1807 had already increased costs of production, and emancipation further increased the shortage of labor, while production was on a steady decline. Furthermore, in 1846, the protective tariff on sugar was removed through the Sugar Equalization Act, abolishing economic protection for the Jamaica's chief export. While this act was ultimately intended to lower the cost of living for the citizens of England, it facilitated the rapid economic decline of the British West Indies. The plantocracy class was ruined as sugar prices dropped rapidly, causing plantations to become abandoned, leaving the formerly enslaved populous to fend for themselves. After the apprenticeship period ended in 1838, many formerly enslaved persons found themselves homeless, receiving the unfortunate news that the homes they had built and the garden plots they cultivated on their masters' property were not theirs and they were ordered to pay rent or move.

In his *Narrative of the Wesleyan Mission to Jamaica*, published in 1849, Peter Duncan describes a tremendous increase of 3,758 members from 1831–1835, the golden years of missionary activity. However, in the closing pages of his book he writes,

> It must however be stated, that the hopes which were cherished and expressed at the District Meeting of 1844 have not been fully realized. The Island was then on the eve of those disastrous changes which have interrupted its civil prosperity and involved so many in poverty and ruin. Vast numbers of the members have suffered and from the abandonment of estates and other causes they have been scattered throughout the Island, in many instances beyond the reach of Christian ministry. The result has been what may be expected, namely a considerable diminution of members since 1844.[62]

---

61. Curtin, *Two Jamaicas*, 168.
62. Duncan, *Narrative of the Wesleyan Mission to Jamaica*, 393–94.

Missionary churches had to grapple with new problems of managing a large, impoverished, uneducated population with inadequate leadership, at a time when the humanitarian interest and financial support to the Jamaican mission was declining from the parent churches in England. Furthermore, most English missionaries could not foresee the problem of forcing acculturation upon African Jamaicans in their most sacred area—their religion—at a time when the tenuous social and economic conditions of nineteenth-century Jamaica presented novel anxieties which reinforced African Jamaican religiosity among the indigenous masses. During the years immediately prior to and immediately after emancipation this problem would become apparent, particularly as African Jamaicans expressed the desire to become leaders within the missionary churches. To their credit, at this time, the Baptists established themselves as the most revolutionary missionary church; the most tolerant of African religious expression, the most socially engaged—implementing a plan of social engineering which assisted the former slaves with fair wage negotiation and provided housing to many homeless peasants by establishing free villages which allowed many persons to buy land at reasonable cost. However, the collapse of the plantation system meant scores of persons became destitute and desperate. None of the missionary churches were socially, culturally, or economically prepared to respond adequately to the societal disarray that followed in the post-emancipatory years. Therefore, the majority of the recently emancipated, but impoverished, persons responded through the socio-cultural institution of religion which had provided consistent security and sanctuary for their oppressed bodies, minds, and spirits. Myalism's notion of sin as sorcery, an offense against communal well-being, as opposed to being antagonistic to God, made it more relevant to most African Jamaicans than any missionary version of Christianity. It was the Native Baptist, Myalist Christians who had assumed a leading role in the major slave rebellion during 1831–1832, prompting it to be called, "The Baptist War." Without question, Native Baptist leaders and their members operated within a unique African Jamaican religious consciousness which provided coherency for their misfortunes in the nineteenth century.

A few years after the abolition of slavery an outbreak of *myalism* occurred on the island. The first identifiable revival of *myalism* was described as "the great myal procession," which occurred within the northwestern parishes of the island, from December 1841 throughout most of 1842. Monica Schuler reports that the deprivation that persons experienced in the northern Jamaican parishes of St. James and Trelawny, positioned it to be the center of Myalism in the 1820s, 1830s, and 1840s. "Since 1838 a number of unexpected deaths had occurred in the Spring estate village; these were ascribed to obeah, which was then blamed for every misfortune. During Christmas of 1841, tenants of Spring invited Myalists from nearby Ironshore estate to cleanse Spring of obeah, and everyone but the Presbyterians in the village participated in the ceremonies."[63] Curtin states that the southeastern part of the island witnessed an outbreak of *myalism* in 1846, while "still other occurrences in the countryside during 1848, 1852, 1860—and in Kingston itself in 1857."[64]

Myal Christianity, in its Native Baptist form, offered rituals, which promised a cure for societal woes. Because misfortune had its roots in the sorcery of *obeah*, society's ills could be reversed by the antisorcery communal ritual of *myalism*. The Native Baptist churches grew rapidly alongside the missionary churches after emancipation, but continued to increase in the 1840s, as the missionary churches declined, as disillusionment and disappointment increased with the gross lack of material security following emancipation. The missionaries had never been a part of the Jamaican powerful elite, therefore they lacked the social status or economic clout to ameliorate the plight of the underclass. The Native Baptists took action in 1840s, their leaders boldly asserted their independence and began to preach hope to the masses using prophetic and millennial language. The message was that they were God's angels, sent by Him to do His work and clear the land for Jesus Christ who would come again soon, to put the world right again. Native Baptist leaders targeted two groups of Europeans—the planters and the missionaries. Planters were targeted for their unjust laws, which oppressed the poor peasant class, and missionaries were targeted for their denouncement of Native Baptist teaching and practices. The upshot is that Native Baptist ideology was a consistent option and, more frequently than not, a spiritual supplement to the missionary Eurocentric worship experience.

The Great Revival Begins

This became vividly apparent in the event recalled as the Great Revival of 1860–61. Jamaica's Great Revival began as an extension of the transatlantic

63. Schuler, "Myalism," 71.
64. Curtin, *Two Jamaicas*, 170.

phenomenon which occurred in America in 1858 and 1859 and in Britain in 1859. These revivals had their theological foundation within North America's eastern states and secured the conquest of Arminianism over Calvinism throughout much of the Protestant English speaking world. The Wesleyan Methodist notion of perfection was conflated with the notion of being born again through an experience of ecstatic religion. Jamaica would not escape the theological ideas taking root in America and England and the enthusiasm of revival was embraced to address the issues of sin and misfortune. The nineteenth-century revival was championed by an ecumenical group of charismatic personalities on both sides of the Atlantic; within North America, Charles Finney, the noted Presbyterian and Phoebe Palmer, a Methodist evangelist, were at the forefront of the religious movement. C.H. Spurgeon, a prominent Baptist in London, was a strong supporter of the Baptist Mission in Jamaica and he travelled to Jamaica in 1859 to preach at Exeter Hall, sharing enthusiastically about the revival simultaneously occurring in England.

The Great Revival began as a Jamaican ecumenical effort, as ministers from the Presbyterian, Baptist, and Methodist missionary churches gathered often to pray and fast for spiritual revitalization to recoup the losses of members, financial support, and religious fervor in the previous two decades. The prayer meetings gradually increased in 1860, until, by April, there were two being held a day, morning and evening. Finally, in mid-October prayerful petition yielded to religious ecstasy among the Moravian congregations in St. Elizabeth. The revival quickly spread through the western part of the island and then travelled eastward along the north and south coasts. By the middle of 1861, the intense religiosity peaked throughout the entire island and it lasted well into 1862. Initially, the missionaries who diligently sought after the revival were extremely pleased. It even gained the recognition of the Anglican clerical leadership as a genuine work of God, however this pleasure was short-lived. The incursions of *myalism* within Christianity, which began in the 1840s, began to boldly enter the orthodox churches, where occasionally, members would become possessed by a spirit during a worship service. These incursions of Africanisms would manifest themselves in ways which were quite disconcerting to pastors unfamiliar with those forms of religious expression. To the consternation of the missionaries, eventually the whole revival became dramatically African in expression, belief and practice.

JAMAICA AND REVIVALISM

There were oral confessions, trances and dreams, 'prophesying,' spirit-seizure, wild dancing, flagellation and mysterious sexual doings that were only hinted at in the missionary reports. One missionary accepted the explanation of a follower that two different spirits were taking possession of the converts—the Spirit of Christ and another, diabolical spirit trying to undo the Divine Work. But there was no getting around it: the Great Revival had turned African. It became more and more a mixture of myalism and Christianity, ending as a permanent addition to the Afro-Christian cults. The [black] revivalists were disowned by those [missionaries] who initiated the movement. The . . . [congregations] dwindled away, leaving the missionaries at the lowest ebb since their decline began.[65]

This episode in Jamaica's history concretized the social tension within the relations between the British missionaries and the poor black masses. Prior to emancipation the missionaries and the enslaved communities were both viewed as antagonists by the ruling plantocracy. However, after emancipation, the socio-cultural dynamic shifted—by the 1860s, the missionaries had become assimilated within Jamaica's dominant white society—and regarded with suspicion by most blacks, although they were the Europeans most interested in the well-being of all members of Jamaican society. Racial conflict began to color every social ill; and, the strange behavior put on display during the revival cultivated general feelings of unease and, in many cases, terror among the whites. Whenever the blacks gathered for a large prayer meeting or the revival drums were heard in a nearby village, the whites quickly passed the word, "The blacks are drilling." The activities and whereabouts of the blacks took on a new sense of mystery and potency, which further deteriorated the social relations between missionaries and the larger black population.[66] The Revival forced the Baptist missionaries from London to make a permanent break between themselves and the Native Baptists. Though the intensity of the Great Revival would eventually subside, the experience of the mass of Jamaicans in a Christian spirituality

65. Curtin, *Two Jamaicas*, 170–71.

66. W.J. Gardner, the author of *The History of Jamaica*, published in 1873, was an eyewitness to the revival activities and documented this oft quoted assessment: "In 1861, there had been a very remarkable religious movement, known as 'the revival.' . . . Like a mountain stream, clear and transparent as it springs from the rock, but which becomes foul and repulsive as impurities are mingled with it in its onward course . . . so with this most extraordinary movement . . . especially . . . where the native Baptists had any considerable influence" (Gardner, *History of Jamaica*, 105).

expressed in African ritual forms became a permanent part of the Afro-Jamaican religious world. "Revival" and "revivalism" came to be the name given and accepted by the congregations dedicated to the experiences of the 1860–62 periods.

Paul Chilcote states in the introduction of his book, *Recapturing the Wesley's Vision,* that whenever he teaches Wesleyan principles on the African continent, he is always impressed at how "Wesley's holism resonates with the African spirit." And particularly as it relates to preaching, that "whenever Word and Spirit come together as God intends, the consequence is liberation. Where the Spirit of the Lord is, there is freedom—freedom from sin, freedom to be, to love, to give and to share. . . . Methodist people witnessed and sang about this kind of liberation."[67] The Native Baptists would interpret this freedom within the context of Jamaican religiosity, in which the liberative witness would be accented with communal rituals which required the drum, the dance, and the oath to concretize their understanding of the importance of subjective agency in a deadly socioeconomic context which perpetually defined them as passive objects.

In revolutionary North America, George Liele was indirectly, yet profoundly, influenced through the preaching of George Whitefield, the architect of the original Methodist Revival, and Liele's conversion and subsequent transmission of an Afro-Baptist faith was reshaped through the power of the preached Word and Spirit in the African Jamaican Native Baptist tradition. The Great Revival transformed Native Baptist tradition into *Revivalism,* a Christian religious ideology, which incorporated *Myal* and *Obeah* cosmology of an active spirit world including ancestral kin, and perpetuated it through communal worship and ritual. In Jamaican Revivalism, the Spirit and the spirits were invoked with the charismatic delivery of the preached Word of God to empower the powerless and equip them with agency and understanding to resist the yokes of sin and oppression.

---

67. Chilcote, *Recapturing the Wesley's Vision,* 12, 34–40.

Chapter Three

BAPTISM, THE WESTERN CHURCH, AND WESLEY

JOHN WESLEY'S PRACTICE AND writings on the sacrament will be presented as evidence and the a foundation for proceeding forward with the central question of the work, namely, how did the history and socio-cultural realities of Jamaica influence the practices of Christian initiation in the early A.M.E. Churches on the island?

Christian Initiation: A Historical Glance at the Practice

The ceremonial use of water is found in most religions and the practice of purification rituals was an inherent part of Judaism, the religion from which Christianity emerged. The biblical evidence, within the synoptic gospels of the New Testament, records that Jesus of Nazareth, a devout Jew upon whom the Christian faith adheres, submitted himself to the baptism of repentance performed by John the Baptist. However, Christian initiation could be said to formally begin with the faith claims stated in the New Testament account of Pentecost, when the Holy Spirit descended upon the apostles gathered in Jerusalem. The Scriptural account in Acts 2 states that the apostle Peter preached the saving act of God through Jesus the Christ to the crowds assembled in Jerusalem for the Jewish feast, and that three thousand were baptized and added to the group of disciples. The New Testament scriptures repeatedly affirm that, as the primitive church expanded, the new converts were taught the gospel of Jesus Christ and then baptized. Further, the earliest extant liturgical document that provides instructions on baptism is the *Didache (The Teaching of the Twelve Apostles* or the "Two Ways").

The socio-historical context of 1820–1920 was a century in which Jamaica faced extreme economic hardship, beginning in the post-emancipation years; vociferous political posturing between Parliament and the local Assembly, which resulted in legislation which added additional strain to social relations already marred by socioeconomic inequity; racial insult and color prejudice between black, white, and colored persons. These external influences created turbulence within all of Jamaica's churches, which blew through the island like the seasonal tropical hurricanes. It is no wonder that the liturgical rite characterized for its importance in the formation of Christian identity should assume a prominent role in the lives of the most vulnerable—impoverished African persons whose sense of self was routinely circumscribed political and socioeconomic forces largely outside of their control.

Furthermore, Jamaica's socio-historical context during 1820–1920 provided a unique environment for the historic theological debate to resume between the pedobaptists, or infant baptism practitioners and the credobaptists, those adhering to the believers' baptist position; the arguments of both positions will be explicated in moderate detail so that the theological presuppositions for both positions can be properly understood before the sociological consequences of liturgical praxis are explored.

Traditional Arguments held for Credobaptism

Credobaptists frequently argue that they are not proponents of adult baptism, but believers' baptism, that conversion, not age, is the criterion for a proper subject of baptism. The ages of believers who are baptized within the African Methodist Episcopal Church span from childhood to senior adulthood. The ritual of baptism serves to ratify the believers' public acts of confession and commitment to the mission of Jesus Christ. The credobaptist position often centers upon the scriptural example of the Philip's baptism of the Ethiopian eunuch found in the New Testament book of Acts. In Acts 8:36, Philip's response to the eunuch's inquiry to what prevented him to be baptized in the presence of a body of water was *"If you believe with all your heart, you may."* The criterion for the credobaptist is *faith*, if the baptismal candidate possesses it, baptism can occur, if faith on the part of the candidate is not present, the ritual must be delayed. The remission of sins is not directly connected to the baptismal act. In this simplistic view, the theological significance for baptism is not viewed in sacramental terms at all. The nature of the ritual is reduced to symbolic terms and as a mere ordinance to be administered in obedience to Jesus the Christ's command.

The credobaptist argument weakens when the notion of covenant theology is introduced. Credobaptists differ among themselves as they approach the study of covenant and its importance within the Christian faith. Scripture within the Old and New Testament reveal covenants that God has entered into with humanity. For example, the Judaic covenant oriented around the notion of circumcision and necessarily involved infants; however, credobaptists counter the notion of the inclusion of infants into the covenant by appealing to the Old Testament book of Jeremiah (Jer 31:31–32) which reveals God's promise to enter into a new covenant with human beings. Christian doctrine has historically taught that the salvific work of Jesus Christ is the fulfillment of that covenant. Though circumcision of male infants was the mark of entry into the old Jewish covenant, there is no indication that the conditions of the New Covenant have the same requirements. In fact, credobaptists utilize Pauline arguments to cite that the reverse is true. Paul uses circumcision as a metaphor to justify the acceptance of Gentiles into the Church. In his Letter to the Romans he states that true circumcision is not something external and physical, but an internal matter of the heart. Credobaptists state that Paul is arguing that spiritual experience, resulting in faith in Christ, is what true circumcision of the New Covenant is about. Baptism accentuates this experience in that the convert has now symbolically died and been raised with Christ.

The definition of the Church is ultimately what is at stake for credobaptists. The fact that many A.M.E. Churches in Jamaica were viewed as 'the Baptist Church' by many persons who reside in the communities in which they originated—is a direct consequence of the way in which they defined themselves as a Christian community of faith. The position that they adopted is that the Church must be composed of professing believers in Jesus Christ.

Credobaptists insist that the connection between the believers' faith and baptism remain essential in order to maintain the integrity of the church and the doctrine of salvation. Credobaptists believe infant baptism removes the criterion of faith from the candidate for baptism and places it upon the parents, guardians, and the church—all of whom may not be sufficient to successfully guarantee that the chronological gap between the act of baptism and the age of accountability will allow the acquisition of faith to occur. Credobaptists state that many baptized infants are not be reared in an environment where faith is allowed to grow, which is why baptism should remain reserved for persons who are converted and are willing to publicly affiliate themselves with the Church by engaging in the work of realizing God's reign on Earth.

Traditional Arguments held for Pedobaptism

In light of the Western Church's embracing of the Augustinian teaching of original sin, even infants require the mercy, forgiveness and salvation of Jesus Christ, and thus need to be reborn through baptism. Parents and guardians are entrusted with sacred responsibility to ensure that children receive the merits of Christ's gracious redemption. The Psalm, "Indeed, I was born guilty, a sinner when my mother conceived me" (Ps 51:5), is an illustrative reminder of the sinfulness of human nature. The notion of ancestral sin begs the question of the importance of baptismal regeneration and John Wesley's understanding of the regenerative character of baptism will be discussed at length in another segment.

However, the dominant European colonizers of the West, who brought their churches to Jamaica, the Spanish clerics of Catholic Church, and the English Anglican churches, were pedobaptists. This is significant for grasping the manner in which marginalized persons who observed its ritual usage may have interpreted the symbols of sacramental power of the church. Most pedobaptist churches support their claim by appealing to biblical evidence that appears to support the practice. There are several instances within the New Testament writings that describe occasions when whole families and households were baptized upon the conversion of the head of household. This scriptural evidence is found primarily within the book of Acts. Acts 11:14 records the baptism of Cornelius and his household; Acts 16:15 describes Lydia's conversion and her baptism along with the rest of her household; Acts 16:33 records the baptism of the Phillipian jailer and his family who was converted when he witnessed the strength of Paul and Silas's faith in prison. Paul's epistle to the Corinthians (1 Cor 1:16) reveals that he had not just baptized Stephanas, the principle convert, but "the household of Stephanas." These scriptures, along with others, are utilized alongside the definition of the term "household" to include infants, children, women and servants, all of who would have been considered dependents and required to obey the decisions made by the head of household in the ancient Roman Empire.

There are several biblical passages within the synoptic gospels that are often used to support pedobaptism which illustrate Jesus' loving relationship with children. Mark 10:13–16, Matthew 19:13–15, and Luke 18:15–17 are parallel passages which relay an incident whereby persons, presumably parents and guardians, are bringing children to Jesus, so that he could lay hands on them and bless them. "The Lucan version is particularly significant, for it makes the point that some, if not all of the children who were brought to Jesus were 'even infants,' a different Greek word being used to describe them from the one translated 'children' in Matthew and Mark."[1]

The historical writings of the Fathers have much to say in support of pedobaptism. Pedobaptists often appeal to Justyn Martyr and Origen to assert the practice in the early church following the apostolic period. In *First Apology*, Justin Martyr referred to the presence of many elderly men and women "who have been disciples of Christ from childhood."[2] Justyn Martyr's writing reveals that baptism in the early church was not exclusively reserved for adults.

Origen's contribution to the church's doctrine is particularly insightful because many of his writings have been preserved, especially his published homilies, which contain strong arguments to justify the practice of infant baptism.[3] Everett Ferguson argues that Origen's defense of the practice of pedobaptism was particularly innovative because he utilized Old Testament passages (specifically Job 14:4–5; Ps 51:5) to explain the presence of corruption of human nature even in infancy—based upon stains received at childbirth, and therefore, extend the baptismal forgiveness of sins to that of washing away ceremonial impurity.[4] With this line of reasoning, Origen contrasts sin with stain and explains that Jesus need purification because of the stain that he received during childbirth. Origen lays the foundation for the church to eventually adopt St. Augustine's doctrine of original sin. Furthermore, Origen is the earliest Church Father to appeal to infant baptism as a custom handed down from the apostles. He appeals to apostolic tradi-

---

1. Bridge and Phypers, *Water that Divides*, 39.

2. Martyr, *First Apology*, 15.6

3. Origen's homilies are preserved largely in a Latin translation by Rufinus. Everett Ferguson cites that those central to Origen's justification of pedobaptism are the *Homilies on Luke* and *Homilies on Leviticus*, which were preached in Caesarea between 231–244.

4. Ferguson, *Baptism in the Early Church*, 368.

tion without citing any references, yet its deployment was a skillful defense for pedobaptism, as John Wesley refers to Origen's claim fifteen centuries later in his similar apology for the practice.

When making the case for pedobaptism, one grapples with the nature of baptism and its impact on the life of an infant or child whose consciousness hasn't fully developed. As stated previously, the traditional pedobaptist approach adheres to the theological position that baptism is a sacrament, and, as such, it has divine intrinsic value within itself. This view defends infant baptism based upon the notion that the outward sign of the ritual, combined with the words of ordained clergy produce the *fact* of an inward change. D.M. Baillie utilizes the sociological concept of environment to indicate that baptism introduces the infant or child into a new environment, that of the Church. The baptized infant is incorporated as a member of the Body of Christ, which provides nurture and communicates the teachings of Christ in a way that leads to future repentance and faith by the baptizand.

Wesley and Infant Baptism

Baillie's theory seems to place the crux of sacramental responsibility upon the Church through its ecclesial pedagogy. Christianity makes the claim that Christ's immediate presence with humanity is through the Holy Spirit's activity within the church. It is expected that the communal practices of the congregation will mold individual character, which reflects Christian virtue. The sacraments are signs and means of accessing Christ's eternal presence in the midst of a gathered congregation, within a particular environmental setting. The development of an infant's human consciousness and volition is dependent upon a supportive Christ-like environment into which the child's rational, spiritual, and emotional life will be socialized. One could put forth the theological position, that the work is all-divine, and that God has already given sufficient grace for admittance into the church. However, from a sociological perspective, it could also be argued that if the ecclesiastical pedagogy is wanting in any respect, the environment established for the nurture of Christian character, may unintentionally fall short of the goal of making disciples.

The simple credobaptists approach avoids this dilemma, but pedobaptists have struggled with this as a reality for centuries. Another ritual was created by the church to counter the perceived dilemma of Roman Catholics and Anglicans (and currently, certain Methodists): the ritual is adopted

BAPTISM, THE WESTERN CHURCH, AND WESLEY

confirmation, a coming of age postbaptismal rite through catechesis, the laying on of hands and full acceptance into the church through the partaking of First Communion.[5] Wesley objected to the performance of the rite, which was regularly practiced within his beloved Anglican Church, as inherited from the Roman Catholic Church. Randy Maddox states that Wesley's aversion to the ritual could be attributed to several factors: *impersonal administration*; the *requirement of a bishop* to perform the chrismation and lay hands; and the *ecclesiastical guarantee of the bestowal and reception of the Holy Spirit* through confirmation.[6]

The most important document on baptism written by John Wesley was "A Treatise on Baptism." It was written in 1756 and published in 1758 as part of the larger work, *A Preservative Against Unsettled Notions in Religions*. Methodist scholars largely concur that Wesley relies heavily upon William Wall, author of *The History of Infant Baptism*, and from a pamphlet previously published by his father, Samuel Wesley in 1700. Wesley introduced his statement of baptism with a definition: "It is the initiatory sacrament which enters us into covenant with God. It was instituted by Christ, who alone has the power to institute a proper sacrament, sign, seal, pledge and means of grace, perpetually obligatory on all Christians."[7] Wesley continued by positioning baptism as the mark of God's new covenant with humanity, just as circumcision was the mark of the previous Mosaic covenant. The materiality of water as a natural cleansing agent, and the insignificance of baptismal mode, takes up the next few paragraphs of "A Treatise on Baptism," as Wesley referred to New Testament scripture to cite that sprinkling or pouring, and not immersion, was probably the preferred mode of baptism in the apostolic church.

Wesley's baptismal theology is presented within five principle benefits that persons receive at baptism. The first benefit is the cleansing away from the guilt of original sin. Wesley's appropriation of the Augustinian concept of humanity's inherited corruption due to the sin of Adam requires a solution. He devoted attention upon this necessity for infants and children in *The Doctrine of Original Sin, According to Scripture, Reason and Experience*. This document states that the divine grace of God has been made available through the atoning work of Christ to free humanity from the state of sinful

---

5. Many Methodist churches no longer withhold Holy Communion from children who have not experienced catechesis.

6. Maddox, *Responsible Grace*, 227.

7. Wesley, *Preservative Against Unsettled Notions*, 143.

oppression. "The virtue of this free gift—the merits of Christ's life and death . . . are applied to us in baptism."[8] The problem lies in attempting to reconcile Wesley's Augustinian beliefs with his theory of prevenient grace and its place in Wesley's economy of salvation. It is difficult to assert that the act of baptism cleanses one of the guilt of original sin, if the presence of Christ's prevenient grace has already neutralized Adamic corruption. Cho presents this is as a theological blind spot for Wesley, in that he never succeeded in logically explicating his understanding of baptism and its relation to prevenient grace. Ole Borgen argues that John Wesley's *ordo salutis* described prevenient grace with components of "natural conscious" and "a measure of free-will supernaturally restored" within humanity, which makes it inapplicable for the unconscious infant and therefore irrelevant in the case of infant baptism.[9]

Baptism's second benefit is that of an initiatory sacrament which provide the means of entry into covenant with God. Daniel Jenkins argues that within the biblical tradition there are numerous scriptural references that relate the creation with that of covenant. The notion of creation and covenant are repeated in such a way as to emphasize the point of divine power constantly bringing order out of, or setting the boundaries of, chaos. The origin of human evil is explained as disobedience to God's commandment, which sets in motion the patterns of systematic destruction into the world.

When a destructive flood destroys the world and seemingly all of God's creation—an episode of grace occurred, which resulted in the Noahic covenant. This covenant is exemplified with the sign of the rainbow, which gives humanity assurance that chaos does not have the ability to overtake humanity and the rest of God's creation. Similarly,

> a covenant of grace is made with Abraham, in which he is promised that the creative power of God will bear work in him and in his seed in a special and purposive way. . . . This covenant is re-affirmed and given concrete expression in the Law which arises out of the miraculous deliverance of the Exodus.[10]

Wesley's covenant theology included the infants and children of baptized persons who have experienced the new birth and are thus living as "new creatures" in Christ Jesus. "Infants are capable of entering into covenant with God, and they have always been included in God's economy of

---

8. Wesley, *Doctrine of Original Sin*, 338.
9. Borgen, *John Wesley on Sacraments*, 127.
10. Moss and Jenkins, "Baptism and Creation," 52.

salvation. Therefore, they have a right to baptism which is the entering seal thereof."[11] John Wesley spent his life's work convincing baptized persons, who were not intentionally working out their soul's salvation, to seek the experience of the new birth. John Parris states that Wesley actively guarded against the concept of a *state* of justification—a fundamental doctrine evident in the principle irresistible grace and election, commonly held by the Puritan divines.[12] Ted Campbell extends this argument by stating that on several points of doctrine, John Wesley's Anglicanism was significantly influenced by Reformed tradition, particularly in sacramental theology. Plainly stated, there was a dimension of sacramental understanding within the Reformed tradition which held that the "moment of regeneration might not be the same moment when the water of baptism was applied."[13] Campbell admits that the main stream of Reformed tradition supported a strong connection between baptism and regeneration, and this is the liturgical understanding that upholds the practice of believer's baptism by immersion in the A.M.E. Church of Jamaica.

Wesley's appropriation of Arminian theology interprets grace to be *resistible*, therefore, justification is merely the door to religion, which swings in two directions and cannot be made secure by a momentary decision. For example, Thomas Langford has argued that prevenient grace should be understood as the gift of God's constant activity in our lives, through which we appropriate forgiveness and spiritual maturation *as we respond* to God's gracious forgiveness and empowerment[14] The baptismal covenant must be constantly affirmed in the present, through constant self-examination and frequent use of the means of grace.

Admission into the visible church is the third benefit of baptism in Wesley's scheme. The church is expected to function as a community of faith, which nurtures the young into spiritual maturity. "Infants ought to come to Christ, and no man ought to forbid them. They are capable of admission into the Church of God. Therefore they are the proper subjects of baptism."[15] Wesley's ecclesiology insists upon the necessity and duty of Christians to utilize the means of grace consistently. Baptism is understood

---

11. Wesley, *Wesley's Works*, 6:16.
12. Parris, *Wesley's Doctrine of Sacraments*, 56.
13. Campbell, *Wesleyan Beliefs*, 52.
14. Langford, "John Wesley's Doctrine," 55–58.
15. Wesley, *Wesley's Works*, 6:18.

as the ordinance instituted by Jesus Christ by which, "in the *ordinary* way, there is no other means of entering into the Church or into heaven."[16]

Wesley's understanding of the Christian community's role of including, sustaining and empowering the Christian supports Baillie's socio-ecclesial assessment of baptism. Both affirm that the Church of God has the mandate to provide baptizands with access to the means of grace alongside intentional religious education. This two-pronged effort sustains a spiritual support system in what may be called the "social work" of the church.

Religious Education for Children

Particularly with respect to Christian nurture of children, John Wesley's mother, Susana Wesley, had no small influence on his view of religious education of children in the Methodist societies. Early on Wesley instructed his preachers to teach and train the children. They were expected to model behavior that revived family worship by instructing parents and children and forming the children into classes within Methodist societies. Wesley often asked his preachers: "Will you diligently instruct the children in every place?"[17] This was followed up with a standardized procedure that was to be used for the instruction of the children in the Societies.

1) Where there are ten children in a Society, meet with them at least an hour every week.
2) Talk with them every time you see any at home.
3) Pray in earnest for them.
4) Diligently instruct and vehemently exhort all parents in their homes.
5) Preach expressly on education.[18]

Wesley imbibed from his mother an understanding of sociological importance that baptism is merely the beginning of a spiritual change within children, which might only be secured within an environment of proper instruction and careful discipline. One must begin to impart Christian principles early, beginning as soon as the child can reason, bending the will by implanting consciousness of parental authority and divine mandate.[19]

---

16. Wesley, *Preservative Against Unsettled Notion in Religion*, 149.
17. Wesley, *Wesley's Works*, 5:223.
18. Wesley, *Wesley's Works*, 5:223.
19. Susanna Wesley, affectionately called the "Mother of Methodism," wrote over thirty letters to John Wesley in which she offered solicited or unsolicited counsel. John

BAPTISM, THE WESTERN CHURCH, AND WESLEY

Wesley believed that children were capable of the same religious experiences as adults, and his journal cites several instances of extraordinary piety in small children. Conversely, "baptized children were also prone to evil tendencies, 'still beset by the diseases of pride, self-will, and love of the world in which they are born.' . . . Therefore the goal or religious training is . . . to make predominant the principle of grace and to overcome the principle of nature. This is to be done, with the help of God, by discipline and teaching."[20] Therefore his writings and sermons often discuss parenting and the importance of religious education in the home:

> Instruct them early, from the first hour that you perceive reason begins to dawn. Truth may begin to shine upon the mind far earlier than we are apt to suppose. And whoever watches the first opening of the understanding, may be little and little, supply fit matter for it to work upon, and may turn the eye of the soul towards good things, as well as towards bad or trifling ones. Whenever a child begins to speak, you may be assured reason begins to work.[21]

Not a parent himself, Wesley could not practice what he preached in the home; however, the school was another institution which should train children to live virtuous lives. The best example of this is in the socio-religious pedagogy of the school he established for young males, Kingswood College. Wesley expected his pupils, ages seven to twelve, to spend much time reading Scripture and in prayer. Alongside religious training, he insisted that they be taught Reading, Writing, Arithmetic, English, French, Latin, Greek, Hebrew, History, Geography, Rhetoric, Logic, Ethics, Geometry, Algebra, Physics and Music.[22] Wesley's religious education curriculum was rigorously employed with the objective of producing pious children whose piety would continue into adulthood, as they assumed their respective roles in society as useful citizens.

The fourth and fifth benefits of baptism, as stipulated by Wesley, are related to the properties of regeneration in the life of the believer. Baptizands are made children of God, and consequently, heirs to the Kingdom

---

Wesley did seek her counsel on the business of child rearing, and Susanna responded from Epworth in July 1732 with an oft cited letter in which she lists the method and 'by-laws' employed in her household. See Charles Wallace Jr.'s published editorial work, Wallace, *Susanna Wesley*.

20. Prince, *Wesley on Religious Education*, 81. This quotation is *about* Wesley, not by Wesley.

21. Wesley, *Wesley's Works*, 2:304.

22. Wesley, *Wesley's Works*, 2:332.

of God. The process of acquiring the characteristics, which constitute divine resemblance befitting children of God, is what regeneration is, and therefore the mere application of water could never do that; hence Wesley argues that the regenerative property of baptism is not through the outward washing of the material substance of water, but by the inward grace which is infused through the sacrament. "Herein a principle of grace is infused, which will not be wholly taken away unless we quench the Holy Spirit of God by long continued wickedness."[23] The previous sentence eloquently summarizes Wesley's Arminian notion of what Maddox calls "responsible grace." Simply put, all grace can be lost if humans fail to receive it and utilize it through faith-filled responses of obedience and service. Particularly as it related to infants and baptismal grace, Wesley believed that it was almost always lost due to willful sin once children reached the age of reason. He says of his own experience, that he thought he had "sinned away the washing of the Holy Ghost" that he received at his own baptism by the time he had reached the age of ten.[24]

As previously stated, Wesley wrote the "Treatise on Baptism" in 1756, two years before it was published in 1758, and he never revised or republished it afterwards. Although there were several baptismal issues where Wesley's views evolved, the one modification that Wesley made to the document just prior to publishing the "Treatise," pertained to a widening of his view on the *proper administrator of the sacraments*. Gayle Felton states, "It was Wesley's definition of valid ordination which changed and not his insistence that only one who has been properly ordained could baptize."[25] While he never endorsed baptism by laity, his acceptance of ministerial orders from other Christian communities of faith, which were not recognized as having connections to Churches who could claim an apostolic inheritance, is an indicator of Wesley's progressive pragmatism and "catholic spirit," which sought to ensure the salvation, cure, and care of souls. His insistence upon baptism being performed by one properly ordained to administer the sacrament was consistent, such that this issue is the only area in which Wesley consents to rebaptism. Charles Wesley records a heated exchange in 1739, between his brother John and the Anglican Bishop of London, on the subject of rebaptism in cases where a layperson had performed the initial baptism. In spite of the Bishop's opposing view (the *Book of Com-*

---

23. Wesley, "Treatise," 149.
24. Charles Wesley's diary in Wesley, *Journal*, s.v. "May 24, 1738."
25. Felton, *This Gift of Water*, 17.

mon Prayer allowed laity to conduct baptisms in case of necessity), Wesley argued that he would continue to rebaptize persons who had previously received lay baptisms at their request.[26]

Other areas in which Wesley's views evolved include that of *proper place* and *proper mode* for baptism. Although the Church of England stipulated for baptisms to occur in the presence of the Church before an assenting congregation, the common practice emerged for baptisms to take place in private homes as situations permitted. This practice emerged undoubtedly due to the high infant mortality rates during the Church's medieval period. Richard Hooker argued for private baptism as a practice:

> If the place appointed for baptism be a part of Christ's institution, it is but an institution of Sacrifice, baptism an institution of Mercy in this case. He which requireth both mercy and sacrifice rejecteth his own institution as sacrifice, where the office of sacrifice would hinder mercy from being shewed.[27]

Wesley's inclinations brought him in line with the rubric in the *Book of Common Prayer* which admonished persons to call upon clergy to perform baptism in the Church. Later, as he would be banned from many Anglican churches, Wesley would administer the rite of sacrament in various and sundry places. Felton records, "By at least 1740, baptisms were often being conducted in the homes of the people. Many were also celebrated at the Foundery in London . . . as he traveled about in England, Wesley . . . baptized wherever the people gathered."[28]

As a young Anglican cleric, especially as a Society for the Propagation of the Gospel (SPG) missionary to Georgia during 1736–37, Wesley had the sacramental praxis of a zealot. He insisted upon immersion; in fact, his unyielding emphasis on trine immersion, as dictated in the 1549 rubric of the *Book of Common Prayer,* caused him no small amount of distress in the Georgia colony. Felton reports that of the ten indictments against him during his troubled ministry, five of them were related to baptism.[29] As reflected within the "Treatise," he would soften his views on the manner of the proper mode of administering the water and would come to view each

---

26. Charles Wesley's diary in Wesley, *Journal,* 2:93.
27. Keble and Walton, *Works of Learned and Judicious Divine,* 280.
28. Felton, *This Gift of Water,* 21.
29. Felton, *This Gift of Water,* 23. Wesley's troubled mission to the American colony is well documented. See Outler, *John Wesley* for a general historical account.

mode as a symbolic representation of Christ's gospel as recorded in the New Testament scripture.

Wesley offered additional commentary on the sacramental act of baptism in *The Sunday Service of the Methodists in North America with other Occasional Services,* which was published in 1784, and written to establish the Methodist Church in North America; seven years before his death. One might surmise that the *Sunday Service* document is representative of Wesley's "settled" thought on the matter. In actuality, Wesley's thought and praxis on the matter of baptism are riddled with complexity and have caused no small amount of confusion within the communions of faith with Methodist heritage. The root cause of the misunderstanding is Wesley's disjointed stance (as an Anglican clergyman) on baptismal regeneration. In both the "Treatise on Baptism" and the *Sunday Service* document, to be used by Methodists in North America, Wesley's terminology reveals his discomfort with the Anglican doctrine of baptismal regeneration. In both manuscripts, he avoids the term *baptismal regeneration*, found in the *Book of Common Prayer,* but simply uses the term regeneration. In his presentation of Article XVII "Of Baptism" in *Sunday Service,* he states that baptism is "a sign of regeneration and the new birth." Furthermore, Wesley is careful in his usage of the term *sacrament* and its derivatives in the hermeneutical tradition of the Anglican Church. With regard to Wesley's theological perspective on the sacraments in Christ's church, Ole Borgen posits that the question, which must be asked, whether Wesley's emphasis upon the sacraments is largely "pragmatic and fragmentary, or whether his theology, and thus also his sacramental theology, is unitive and systematic and not incidental and disconnected."[30]

Borgen's question marks the faultline of the center of baptismal controversy that often sends tremors through the Methodist ecclesial church family. Scholars and church leaders have analyzed his writings and practices on baptismal regeneration and the nature and function of the sacrament, only to draw conclusions that are often situated on opposite sides of the liturgical and doctrinal spectrum. There are those who take the position that Wesley's avoidance of the term "baptismal regeneration" and cautionary use of the term, "sacrament," indicates an extreme stance against any *ex opere operato* interpretation of the rite of baptism in either its infant or adult form.[31] Nineteenth-century scholars of Methodism, such as T.G. Wil-

---

30. Borgen, *Wesley on Sacraments,* 47.

31. *Ex operate operato* represents the highest form of sacramentalism in which the

liams and William Cannon, would fall in this category; Cannon actually concluded that Wesley broke away from the Church of England on the matter of baptismal regeneration.[32] Opponents of the dominant view of Wesley's evangelicalism include John Parris, Luke Tyerman, and Ole Borgen, all of whom vehemently uphold the sacramental significance of baptism for Wesley and emphasize the objective grace conveyed in the sacrament.

Wesley's words and practice illustrate a circumscribed, yet balanced synthesis between sacramentalism and evangelicalism as it relates to baptism. He utilizes the Church of England's definition as that of a visible means of grace, ordained by God to be performed in Christ's church. A sacrament consists of two parts: the *signum*, the outward material sign, and the *res*, the inward, spiritual grace, which is being signified. However, his sermon "The New Birth" makes it clear that the sacrament of baptism and the "new birth" are not the same thing. In this sermon, he uses a portion of the Anglican definition of baptism as cannon fodder to explode his critique of universal baptismal regeneration. "'What is the inward part or thing signified? A death unto sin and a new birth unto righteousness.' Nothing therefore is plainer, according to the Church of England, that baptism is not the new birth."[33] Bernard Holland argues that Wesley upheld that baptismal regeneration occurred during infant baptism, which was obligatory to negate original sin, but, because baptismal regeneration was almost certainly lost because of the habitual occurrence of willful sin, once one reached the age of reason, a second regeneration called the new birth, should be experienced as a subjective change of will. Ole Borgen argues against Holland's argument, as it assumes that the majority, if not all persons baptized as infants inevitably lose the regenerating grace of baptism.[34] Gayle Felton states that Wesley's personal experience led him to concur that baptismal grace was usually lost, and therefore a subsequent experience of regeneration was necessary "without denying the validity of the sacramental rebirth."[35] Campbell presents an interpretation of Wesley's sacramental

---

baptismal ritual in itself is ascribed objective potency from God. Puritans critiqued this as a form of paganism and magic within the church, however it was this ideology that provided a foundation for Martin Luther, who often gained spiritual fortitude by remembering his baptism, and taught others to do the same.

32. Williams, *Methodist and Anglicanism*, 42.
33. Wesley, "New Birth," 12.
34. Holland, *Baptism in Early Methodism*, 56–59.
35. Felton, *This Gift of Water*, 41.

understanding in which regenerative baptismal grace need not accompany the application of water to be effective in the life of the believer.[36]

The end result was a practical adoption by Wesley, of a two-part interpretation of regeneration, which fit into his soteriological perspective. After studying the progression of Wesley's practices and writings on baptism, from a young Anglican churchman to an elder statesman of an established Methodist movement/Church; this writer has concluded that pragmatism must necessarily support theological arguments that attempt to articulate Wesley's theory of baptismal regeneration. Wesley was always concerned with the end result of outward and inward holiness, i.e., love of God and love of neighbor exhibited in tangible, and sacramental, ways.

With this consideration, this work responds to Borgen's inquiry concerning Wesley's sacramental theology (as it is often exhibited in the A.M.E. Church in Jamaica) with an illustration that reveals its unconventional nature, while presenting it as unitive toward a pragmatic end.[37] Albert Outler termed John Wesley a "folk-theologian," which in no wise diminished his importance as a major theologian, but created a distinction between normative systematic theology and pastoral folk theology, which is practical and useful for the direct spiritual formation of Christians.[38] The pragmatism, which profoundly influenced Wesley's ministry in doctrine *and* praxis, may be elucidated best through sociological deliberation. One cannot engage in full reflection upon Wesley's view of infant baptismal regeneration without recalling the fact that nine of his siblings died as infants. He was among ten children who reached adulthood out of a total of nineteen children born to his parents, the Rev. Samuel and Susanna Wesley. Infant mortality is the single most important reason that Everett Ferguson ascribes to the original rise of infant baptism in the Early Church.[39]

---

36. Campbell, *Wesleyan Beliefs*, 49–52.

37. See Borgen, *Wesley on Sacraments*, 26–27.

38. Outler, *John Wesley*, 1–33.

39. Ferguson, *Baptism in the Early Church*, 372. Ferguson's list of the probabilities contributing to the origin of infant baptism include: Jewish proselytism and the solidarity of the family unit in ancient societies, the acceptance of original sin as doctrine, the initiation of children in mystery religions, and the old Punic practice of child sacrifice. However, using the evidence of the earliest extant Christian inscriptions of the late second century and early third century, Ferguson cites that the prevalence of emergency baptisms demonstrated towards dying children is very telling, as there was no evidence that infants were routinely baptized after birth in the early church. As demonstrated, Wesley's eighteenth-century baptismal theology included a firm grasp of original sin and his personal experience and social context was one in which infant mortality was widely

BAPTISM, THE WESTERN CHURCH, AND WESLEY

As an academically trained folk theologian in the Church of England, John Wesley understood from scripture, reason, and experience that original sin corrupted human nature from conception and that infant baptism was the ordinary way in which the church conferred God's gracious remedy for humanity's inherent corruption.[40] The performance of personal, actual willful sin, which occurred with the development of human consciousness, demanded a personal, willful act of submission and cooperation with the spiritual therapy of God's grace. In the early church, this actual willful act of submission and cooperation was generally symbolized through the sacrament of baptism. The majority of members in Methodist societies had received infant baptism and, as long as the administrator of the rite possessed the ecclesiastical qualifications, Wesley held that they had been properly initiated into Christ's church. However, he insisted upon the use of the means of grace at every opportunity—for the renewal or the deepening of the baptismal covenant.[41] Wesley's practical insistence upon the power, rather than the form of religion, found expression in the love feasts, the class and band meetings, acts of social holiness, and the preached word. In fact, this pragmatism is what has allowed the Methodist church to progress in various cultural contexts and geographic regions, as David Hempton so ably illustrates. In this vein, I respond to Borgen's inquiry, with a statement which posits that a Wesleyan understanding of regeneration as practiced within most early Jamaican A.M.E. Churches was pragmatic and unitive, in the manner in which its unique contextual history, sociological *and* theological matters are given consideration. The analogy that Richard Heitzenrater offers of Wesley, as a swordsman who shifts his theological weight according to the direction of the argument, is very useful as one considers baptism in Wesley's thought and practice. The sociological consideration is of prime consideration as one reflects upon the differences of societal structure and social relations in eighteenth-century England versus those of the mid-nineteenth and early twentieth centuries in Jamaica. This deliberation necessarily includes a closer examination of ritual and its symbolic use of

---

prevalent.

40. The longest document ever written by John Wesley was a 506-page document titled *The Doctrine of Original Sin according to Scripture, Reason, and Experience*, published in 1757. He would subsequently republish Part One of the document as "A Sermon on Original Sin" numerous times from 1759 through 1788.

41 Holland, *Baptism in Early Methodism*, 47. Bernard Holland argues that Wesley believed that baptism was just one of several means by which God's "preventing, justifying, or sanctifying" grace could be conveyed to the faithful.

language and action, which provide semiotic tools for the restoration of the relationships between humanity and God through the merits of Christ.

John Wesley's England was largely a society that was monolithic in language and culture. The distinctions were largely attributed to lack of wealth or social status. The poor English colliers, who were most affected and responsive to John Wesley's message of The New Birth, received spiritual affirmation from the Methodist societies that convinced them of their human worth. Over time, this spiritual affirmation gradually became social affirmation with material comforts and respectability. Wesley never emphasized baptism as a requirement for membership among the Methodists.[42] It is the aim of the next chapter to illustrate that while the Wesleyan requirement was altered in the teaching and practice of Christian initiation in early Jamaican A.M.E. Churches, the two-fold regeneration upholds Wesley's soteriological understanding. To demonstrate this to this end, we must analyze the relationship between conversion and ritual in the socio-historical context of Jamaica. It is hopeful that the socio-historical considerations that influenced the trajectory of Wesleyan thought, as viewed through Jamaican popular religiosity in the early A.M.E. Church, will support this claim. The missionaries who preached and taught the gospel of Christ through Methodism and African Methodism would quickly make this discovery and they worked among the enslaved and colonized persons of African descent. Rev. Thomas Pennock and Rev. Alfonso Dumar are important personalities, whose missionary efforts bear witness to the sociological and cultural concerns that the Wesleyan Methodist and African Methodist missionaries faced in Jamaica during the century of 1820–1920; just before and after emancipation, through the early twentieth century prior to World War I.

---

42 There was only one condition required for persons who desired admission into a Methodist society: "A desire to flee from the wrath to come, and to be saved from their sins."

Chapter Four

METHODIST MISSIONS AND BAPTIST RESISTANCE

THIS CHAPTER AIMS TO demonstrate how independent Christian communities, formed by enslaved Africans in the nineteenth-century British colony of Jamaica, utilized the baptismal mode of immersion as a convincing and effective ritual performance for the purpose of affirming their humanity, resisting oppression and creating a new Christian identity. This preferred mode could be recast as a new modality of creative thought by the descendants of Africa, who, in the vein of Charles Long's thought—utilized the ritual to reorient themselves in 'how one comes to terms with the ultimate significance of one's place in the world."[1] The ministry of Rev. Thomas Pennock, a Wesleyan Methodist Missionary to Jamaica in the nineteenth century, will be employed to analyze the rite of baptism and its sociological and theological importance within popular African Jamaican religiosity. Second, the initiation rite in traditional African religion will be briefly referenced to validate the claims made regarding the process of identity formation. The weakening of the use of initiation rites in the black Atlantic world is presented as justification to effort to understand with the important role of initiation in Christianity, namely the rite of baptism in Native Baptist communities within nineteenth-century Jamaica.[2]

---

1. Long, *Significations*, 7.
2. The replacement of African culture and tradition with Christian beliefs, myths, and rituals in the New World is called "the death of the gods" by Albert Raboteau in *Slave Religion*.

REBAPTISM CALMLY CONSIDERED

Thomas Pennock, WMMS missionary in Pre-Emancipation Jamaica

The case of the Reverend Thomas Pennock, a Wesleyan Methodist Missionary to Jamaica, provides an interesting example of how an English clergyman made the necessary adjustments to conduct meaningful ministry in the humid and hostile climate of nineteenth-century Jamaica. His experience is one that is uniquely significant and useful for displaying the manner in which cultural contact in the nineteenth-century Jamaican social context transpired. The presentation of socio-historical information will be useful as an illustration of the contrasts between British Methodism and indigenous Jamaican religiosity. Moreover, an analysis of Pennock's correspondence to the Wesleyan Methodist Missionary office, in the light of the socio-historical complexities of nineteenth-century Jamaica, should provide insight on the doctrinal dispute that Pennock raised with regard to the Methodist doctrine of infant baptism.

From the time John Wesley wrote that the slave trade was "the execrable sum of all villainies," British Methodists vigorously championed the abolitionist cause in England. However, Wesleyan Methodist missionaries during the pre-emancipation period of the West Indies were often recipients of the brute force of the opposition from slave owners while serving in the colonial mission fields. Missionaries were thus trained to remain politically neutral in the various mission fields throughout the Caribbean. Their job was to convert the souls of men and women and not become entangled in temporal affairs. According to *Hill's Arrangement*, Thomas Pennock entered the ministry in 1818, and began his work as a missionary to the West Indies in St. Kitts, also formally called St. Christopher, in 1819.[3] He itinerated for ten years in various Caribbean islands before returning to England to serve at Durham briefly in 1828. In 1829, he was reassigned and stationed in the Jamaica District. By 1830, he was the minister at Parade Chapel in Kingston and held the position of Chairman of the Jamaica District.

Jamaica had always been the most difficult assignment in the West Indies for missionaries. Thomas Coke, founder of Methodist missions, quickly collided with the entrenched power of pro-slavery plantation owners. From the time of Coke's initial sermon to the ministry of William Hammet (the

---

3. Hill, *Alphabetical Arrangement of Wesleyan Methodist* (2nd ed.) 90; Hill, *Alphabetical Arrangement* (3rd ed.), 108; Hill, *Supplement to Hill's Alphabetical Arrangement*, 46. The fourth edition of *Hill's Arrangement* lacks an entry for Rev. Thomas Pennock. It was published in 1838 and Pennock had left the Wesleyan Methodist Missionary Society by then.

METHODIST MISSIONS AND BAPTIST RESISTANCE

first assigned missionary to Jamaica) and the building of the first chapel on the island, conflict ensued. Findlay and Holdsworth state, "Methodism awakened a vehement resistance in the forces of evil entrenched in that place. The success or failure of the Mission turned upon the vindication of its Gospel in Jamaica." As the largest and most economically viable island in the British West Indies, "Jamaica was the strong hold of the slave-holding interest. . . . Kingston, more than any other spot, was the strategic point of the contention for evangelical truth and religious liberty in the West Indies."[4]

In Jamaica, Methodist chapels were often closed, ministers frequently jailed, and members of Methodist societies were constantly under threat of flogging or imprisonment for insubordination to local authorities. The following exchanges provide an account of the scrutiny Wesleyan Methodists and Baptists were subject to in nineteenth-century Jamaica. The missionaries of these dissenting groups were summoned and asked to testify as "Evidence Before a Commission of Enquiry." In early December 1827, numerous examinations under oath were taken before a committee appointed by the Jamaica Assembly to inquire and report the names of all sectarians or dissenters licensed to preach, teach and reside in Jamaica. These hearings were designed first of all to ascertain the authorized from the unauthorized (the Native Baptist) dissenting preachers and teachers. Secondly, the commission sought to comprehend the economic impact of the dissenters—persons were queried about funds the sectarian churches received from slaves, or members of their various churches and societies, as well as determining in what manner the monies were distributed.

> Question: What is your name: Are you a Wesleyan-Methodist missionary: How long have you resided in Jamaica: Are you duly licensed to preach and teach, and at what place or places do you now preach or teach?
>
> Answer: Peter Duncan is my name. I am a Wesleyan-Methodist missionary. I have resided in Jamaica almost seven years. I am licensed to preach at Grateful-Hill, in St. Thomas's in the Vale, and Unity, in St. Andrew's.
>
> Q: What is the number of your congregation, and of what description of people does it consist, whether of free people or of slaves, or of both?
>
> A: At Grateful-Hill nearly four hundred: at Unity one hundred eighty. They consist of white, free, and slaves.

4. Findlay, *Wesleyan Methodist Missionary Society*, 2:64.

> Q: Do you know of any class of unlicensed persons who travel about the country misleading the slaves, under the pretext of instructing them in religion?
>
> A: I have heard of unlicensed persons, both free and slaves, but do not know any who go about and preach and teach.[5]

Mary Sutliff, a free colored woman who was a Methodist Class Leader partook in one of the lengthier exchanges. The line of questioning took a slightly different turn, in that the examiner took upon himself the subject of proselytization between Baptists and Methodists.

> Q: Do your society make any converts from the Baptist missionaries' congregations, and do they also make converts from those who have become members of your society?
>
> A: If any Baptist has been publicly expelled from their society, we would not receive them; but any that object to rebaptism, or like our mode of worship better, we receive them. One has applied to me to be admitted into my class.
>
> Q: Do you intend it to be understood that slaves never contribute or make offerings of poultry, provisions, &c. for the use of the society, and are such offerings never furnished in kind to the minister, or converted into money for the use of the society?
>
> A: No; not to the best of my knowledge.[6]

Mary Sutliffe's testimony highlights the practice of rebaptism alongside implications for the relationship between Methodists and Baptists in pre-Emancipatory Jamaica.[7]

Thomas Pennock assumed leadership of the Wesleyan Methodists in Kingston, at one of the most contentious times in Jamaica's pre-emancipation history. Upon assumption of his post, he began an apologetic campaign for the Wesleyan Methodist Missionary cause, publishing a pamphlet titled, *Charges Alleged Against the Sectarians by Certain Senators in the*

---

5. WMMS, *Missionary Correspondence*, Box 204, mf. 2224, 417. In 1849, Peter Duncan would publish *A Narrative of the Wesleyan Mission to Jamaica*, a useful account of his missionary service in Jamaica.

6. WMMS, *Missionary Correspondence*, Box 204, mf. 2224, 409.

7. The relationship between Methodists and Baptists has always involved tension as it relates to rebaptism. John Wesley's sermon, "A Catholic Spirit" from 2 Kings 10:15, was his attempt to generate ecumenical goodwill without compromise to the essentials of Christianity. This sermon addresses the Baptists in this manner, "I believe infants ought to be baptized, and that this may be done either by dipping or sprinkling. If you are otherwise persuaded, be so still, and follow your own persuasion." See Outler and Heitzenrater, *John Wesley's Sermons*, 305.

METHODIST MISSIONS AND BAPTIST RESISTANCE

House Assembly on the 30th of November 1830, Examined and Refuted. In this pamphlet, Pennock vigorously addresses charges of religious enthusiasm, robbing the slaves, and the most dangerous of all, that of provoking insubordination among the enslaved population and the freed persons of color. He concluded with the statement:

> Methodism is Christianity, the epitome given above of its doctrine and discipline prove to demonstration. They prove that the system of Methodism is derived from the Word of God, the sacred fountain of infallible And eternal truth. I do not say that Methodism is Christianity to the destruction of any other sect, by no means, For I believe that many other denominations can support their claims to the illustrious title.... With this explanation then, allow me again to say that Methodism is Christianity, in consequence of which we can in common with Other branches of the Christian Church, claim our part in the divine promises, ... which will be fulfilled, and despite every obstacle, the glory of the Lord shall be fulfilled, and all flesh shall see it together, for the mouth of the Lord hath spoken it (Isa 40). Methodism is helping forward the onward spread of this glory, and doing her part in evangelizing the world, and while God is her refuge and strength as He has ever been, no human or hellish power will be permitted to paralyze her, hitherto, conquering arm, quench the ardour of her zeal, impede the progress of her operations, or tarnish the luster of her shining glory, but she will under the divine blessing triumphantly go forward, cooperating with her sister Churches until the grand result of their untied operations, is the spiritual subjugation of the kingdoms of this world.[8]

Unfortunately for Pennock and the other Nonconformist missionaries, the largest slave insurrection occurred a year later. On 25 December 1831, the Christmas Rebellion or, as is commonly called, the Baptist War began. Historians credit Samuel Sharpe an enslaved, literate Baptist class leader in the Rev. Thomas Burchell's congregation with planning the Christmas Rebellion at his weekly prayer meetings.[9] Sharpe was an elo-

---

8. Pennock, "Charges alleged against the Sectarians," 40–41. This handwritten pamphlet does not indicate its publisher, however it was publicly advertised to a wide audience in the December 1, 1830, issue of the *Jamaica Watchman* newspaper.

9. Cox, *History of Baptist Missionary Society*, 182. While Sharpe was a member of Burchell's officially recognized Baptist Missionary Church, there is overwhelming evidence that substantiates the fact that he had close relationships with Native Baptist leaders and congregations. These relationships allowed the communication of the uprising to be so effective that the rebellion was ascribed to be fully under the control of the Native

quent, charismatic preacher who championed abolition, frequently using the text, "No man can serve two masters," to negate the right of whites to hold blacks in bondage. This scripture quickly became a mantra among the enslaved population.[10] Sharpe knew of the heated abolitionist proceedings occurring in London, and mistakenly believed that emancipation had already been decreed by the British Parliament, but was being withheld by the local plantocracy.[11] He organized a peaceful strike across most sugar estates in western Jamaica during the most critical time for the plantation owners—the time of harvesting the sugar cane. After the Christmas holidays, when the harvesting of the sugar cane was to begin, the slaves were to sit down and tell the planters that they would not begin work without compensation.

> The first oath, to take action to secure the freedom which they thought the British Government had already granted, was taken at a meeting on the Retrieve estate in August 1831. . . . The final planning took place . . . at a meeting of the drivers from the estates concerned in the plot; at this meeting they further "kissed the Book not to hurt any minister." . . . The inclusion of oaths in the developing plans was in accordance with Native Baptist African Jamaican religiosity. Sam Sharpe and his followers certainly found their oaths binding enough to resist belated missionary attempts at the Christmas services to persuade the slaves not to strike.[12]

Dianne Stewart argues that the inclusion of the oath alongside the presence of the Holy Bible as sacred witness demonstrates the presence of the dual value system (African spirituality and European Christianity) present in the Native Baptist theological perspective, in which African spiritual values were given primacy.[13] Sharpe's peaceful work stoppage quickly erupted in violent, destructive behavior when planters began to retaliate. Crops were burned and hundreds were killed, among the dead were fourteen whites. The Jamaican military put down the rebellion after two weeks, and Sharpe and the other leaders of the resistance were executed in 1832.

Baptists. See Curtin, *Two Jamaicas*, 85–86.

10. Turner, *Slaves and Missionaries*, 154.

11. Cox, *History of the Baptist Missionary Society*, 182. Cox writes that Sharpe stated that he knew that the slaves had already been emancipated. Sharpe is quoted as having said, "I know we are free; I have read it in the English papers. I have taken an oath not to work after Christmas, without some satisfaction, and I *will not*."

12. Gordon, *God Almighty Make Me Free*, 98.

13. Stewart, *Three Eyes for the Journey*, 104.

METHODIST MISSIONS AND BAPTIST RESISTANCE

Sharpe's final speech records his urgent desire for freedom. "All I wished was to be free," he stated. "All I wished was to enjoy that liberty which I find in the Bible is the birthright of every man."[14] Sharpe understood freedom from the Bible as an idea that neither blacks nor whites were permitted to hold one another in bondage. Orlando Patterson argues that freedom is a tripartite value that was initially constructed by persons in a condition of enslavement. Patterson presents the Pauline intellectual contribution to Christianity and its process of redemption as a means to forge a spiritual consciousness which emboldens converts to struggle against the forces that enslave them. Emancipation thus becomes an active principle for the Christian, such that he writes to the Phillipian church that they must, "work out [their] own salvation with fear and trembling."[15] Accordingly, the Native Baptist inspired rebellion resulted in two detailed parliamentary inquiries which arguably contributed to the 1833 Abolition of Slavery across the British Empire.[16] Sharpe's resistance demonstrates how the appropriation of the egalitarianism of Christianity was linked with political sensibilities honed in independent Native Baptist churches and their urgent desire for freedom.[17] The English Baptists and Wesleyan Missionaries were viewed as the principal instigators of the rebellion. In the opinion of their owners, the slaves were incapable of carrying out such a detailed

---

14. Gordon argues that the notion of freedom for enslaved Jamaicans had its roots in African religions (Gordon, *God Almighty Make Me Free*, 54). However, the emotive preaching of the Afro-American Baptist preachers who presented the message of the Christian doctrine of salvation to Jamaican slaves was inseparably linked with the Pauline notion of freedom. Scripture provided language through which the desire for freedom was articulated.

15. Patterson, *Freedom*, 1:315. Patterson argues that while Christianity, in its early forms, valued freedom, it was Paul's version of Christianity that completely related the actual experience of freedom with the release from slavery.

16. Mary Turner argues that the British missionaries who provided ministry in pre-emancipation Jamaica were simply catalysts. They "worked in a society where the people had made their own struggle for freedom, under their own leaders, and had pushed their country into the revolutionary mainstream of the time, the struggle for individual liberty sanctioned by law" (Turner, *Slaves and Missionaries*, 202).

17. Patterson, *Freedom*, 3–5. Patterson's three-fold description of freedom is: Personal freedom, the most elementary understanding of liberty, in which a person has a sense that he or she "is not being coerced or restrained by another in doing something desired, and that one can do as one pleases, *insofar as one can*. . . . Sovereignal freedom emerged in the Western world and is simply the power to act as one pleases, regardless of the wishes of others. . . . Lastly, Civic freedom is that of the capacity of adult members of a community to participate in its life and governance."

and destructive plot on their own. Charges were brought against Baptist and Wesleyan missionaries in journals hostile to the missionary cause.[18] Henry Bleby, a Wesleyan missionary who would be assigned to the Falmouth mission on the north coast of the island, describes the plantocracy reaction to the sectarian preachers. "The Baptist chapel at Falmouth was first demolished, after which the Methodist chapel, a handsome building, which had just been put in complete repair, followed the same fate.... The demolition of the Falmouth chapel was speedily followed by the burning of the chapels at Stewart Town in Trelawney and Ebenezer chapel in St. Ann's. At St. Ann's, Ocho Rios, and Oracabessa, chapels were either pulled down or burnt."[19]

As Chairman of the Jamaica District, Pennock communicated these events to the Mission House in London, through the *Wesleyan-Methodist Magazine*. "When and how the awful affair will terminate is hard to say or imagine. In consequence of inflammatory articles which have appeared in the infamous *Courant,* our lives have been and are still in imminent danger; but the power of God and consciousness of our own innocence support our minds in the midst of danger."[20] He vigorously defended his ministers by making appeals before the Governor of Jamaica to secure their physical safety and that of their families. Pennock had to rely upon the numbers of black and colored members of the Methodist societies to secure protection for the property that belonged to the Wesleyan Methodist Missionary Society. Black and colored members often slept in chapels at night and kept watch by day to ensure that inflamed mobs did not accomplish their destructive goals. He also wrote many refutations against these charges in *The Jamaica Watchman*, the newspaper owned by Edward Jordan, a colored man who was a respected member in the Kingston Methodist society.

The following excerpt is one of many of Pennock's submissions, dated May 11, 1832:

> At a meeting of the WESLEYAN MISSIONARIES, and of the leaders of their respective Societies, in this island, convened by the Chairman of and held in the Parade Chapel this 10th Day of May, 1832 for the purpose of PROTESTING against the Report of the Committee, appointed by the Honorable House of Assembly to

18. The *Cornwall Courier* and the *Jamaica Courant* were the newspapers frequently utilized to articulate the planters viewpoint.

19. Bleby, *Death Struggles of Slavery*, 150–51.

20. Extract of a Letter from Mr. Pennock, dated, Kingston, January 16th, 1832, published in *Wesleyan-Methodist Magazine*, April 1832, 296.

> ascertain the causes of the late REBELLION, It was unanimously ... resolved that as neither the Wesleyan Missionaries, nor the Leaders in their societies were directly or indirectly concerned in instigating, or in any way aiding in the late rebellion, we consider the aforesaid Report, as far as it relates in the Wesleyan Methodists, utterly false and unfounded; nearly all the "leaders" being respectable Free Persons, most of whom are owners of Slaves.... We feel ourselves called upon to maintain that our system is ... peculiarly calculated to promote peace and good order among all classes of His Majesty's subjects, whether free or slaves.... Therefore, the aforesaid Report is a gross calumny, not only upon ourselves, and people in this island, but also upon the body, to which we belong.[21]

Although the Jamaica militia had put down the rebellion and martial law had been ended by February 1832, in January 1833, slave owners, dissatisfied with the state of affairs, formed a group called the "The Colonial Church Union (CCU)." Its organizational cover was that of a religious organization led by Anglican clergymen and other leading members of the Church of England, and the intention was to establish branches of the organization in every parish.[22] The Jamaican newspaper *The Courant*, was the principal forum for the expression of anti-missionary views, while solidly supporting the perspective of the plantocracy. Their formal objective was to prepare a petition to the Jamaica Legislature for the expulsion of sectarian missionaries from the island; to instill more rigid discipline among the slaves; and publish a periodical for the rebuttal of every statement that opposed the continuance of slavery.

The CCU's informal objective was carried out by the vicious beating and murder of hundreds of slaves, the incarceration of many Baptist and Methodist missionaries, and the destruction of numerous chapels, mostly Baptist, but some Wesleyan chapels were severely damaged. The intensity of the CCU's wrath was conducted by mobs which were allowed free reign on the north side of the island. After being assigned to Falmouth in April 1832, Henry Bleby and his wife were tarred, feathered, and barely escaped being set ablaze at the hands of a murderous gang in Trelawny.[23]

In Kingston, the CCU's plot became known in advance so guards were placed at the Wesleyan and Baptist chapels. The mayor of the city also provided civic guards to prevent the destruction of further property. In August

21. Pennock, untitled article in *Jamaica Watchman*, May 11, 1832, 8.
22. Curtin, *Two Jamaicas*, 87–88.
23. Bleby, *Death Struggles of Slavery*, 198–204.

1833, the Emancipation Act was passed by Parliament and the pro-slavery forces were summarily defeated. However,

> slave-owning planters in the West Indies lobbied to postpone freedom for adults for twelve years in a form of indenture. Enslaved children under the age of six were emancipated by the new law on 1 August 1834, but older children and adults had to serve a period of bonded labour or "indentured apprenticeship."[24]

The apprenticeship period resulted in substantially more work for Wesleyan missionaries, as recently "freed" slaves were expected to become literate and acquire manners and morality befitting their status as British subjects. In other words, they were expected to become quickly acculturated within acceptable English social mores. Not surprisingly, the apprenticeship period was largely disastrous from the outset. There was no precedent for it and the former slaves could not understand the ambiguous condition between being enslaved and being free. A paraphrase commonly attributed to a Jamaican slave describes their position: "When God freed the slaves in Egypt were they freed or were they made apprentices?" Nevertheless, the Wesleyan Missionaries were vigorously employed, as the principal persons expected to do the work of converting and educating the newly formed apprentice population.

In this vein, Pennock's sermon is quite telling as to how he assumed this charge. In *A Sermon to the Apprentices on the First Anniversary of their Freedom from Slavery*, on the 2nd of August 1835, Pennock made his case. Using the text of 1 Peter 2:11–17, Pennock first refuted the claim that "Christianity makes persons dissatisfied with their lives and prone to rebellion."[25] Next he defined Christian Religion as derived from the "Word of God of the OT and NT."[26] Having established this claim to scriptural infallibility, he emphasized the importance of "good conduct" by Christians. This conduct is described primarily in the human relationships between subject and king and masters and servants. However, Pennock employed this hermeneutical skill to drive the point that "the chief end is to put to silence ignorant and ungodly men."[27]

In the sermon, Pennock described freedom through Christ as one of a spiritual character, freedom from sin and guilt, not freedom from obedience

---

24. Stewart, *Religion and Society*, 75.
25. Pennock, *Sermon to the Apprentices*, 1.
26. Pennock, *Sermon to the Apprentices*, 2.
27. Pennock, *Sermon to the Apprentices*, 2–3.

to God's commands and human ordinances.²⁸ Pennock's description of freedom was of the utmost importance in the Wesleyan sense because, he contended, "this destroys antinomianism." His work concludes with the practical means of the sermonic application: the intention to "impress the precepts upon the minds of the apprentices to continue in their state of probationary freedom, by waiting with patience and proving themselves worthy of complete liberty."²⁹ Pennock's next point illuminated his position on race and society in general. He stated that he detested racial prejudice, and that all men deserved honor, regardless of their skin color. He indicates that God's providence and social order dictate the type of respect persons are due, based upon their, "office, rank, situation, and circumstances of life."³⁰ This statement appears innocuous; however, beginning in 1833, Pennock had begun to be viewed as a radical by his Wesleyan Methodist colleagues, because of his refusal to be silenced on matters of color prejudice in the Wesleyan mission.

During the pre-emancipation period, resentment among black and colored Methodists escalated against Wesleyan Methodist Missionary leadership. Two factors in particular fueled this resentment, the slow promotion of colored ministers and overwhelming opposition to the marriage of white English ministers to colored women. With the end of slavery, these issues came to a head rapidly and eventually burst into a two-phased secession movement; the first was led by Edward Jordan in 1834, a colored publisher and politician, the second would be led by Thomas Pennock in 1837.³¹ In July 1834, the Missionary Committee in England received an anonymous and undated letter from Jamaica. The letter was written specifically to support the charges of racial prejudice in the case of Mr. Walters, a missionary who was ostracized and denied a ministerial assignment because of his engagement to a woman of color. Pennock defended Walters and another missionary by the name of Rowden, who had a romantic interest in a woman of color.³² Pennock had been overruled at a district meeting of 1834 in his defense of Walters. This matter and his contradictory position on the Jamaica Districts' decision to deny Mr. T. E. Ward (a colored Methodist leader) the right to become a full minister placed him on the

28. Pennock, *Sermon to the Apprentices*, 13.
29. Pennock, *Sermon to the Apprentices*, 14.
30. Pennock, *Sermon to the Apprentices*, 22.
31. Stewart, *Religion and Society*, 75
32. Stewart, *Religion and Society*, 77

margins of respectability within the Wesleyan Methodist Missionary social circle. Thomas Pennock, by all accounts, was ahead of his time with regard to his perspective on equal human rights for people of color as it related to their leadership ability, intellectual capacity, and moral fortitude within the Methodist societies.

> By 1834, the stressors of the Wesleyan Methodist Chairmanship in Jamaica had taken tremendous toll on Pennock and his family. His missionary correspondence documents his constant defense of the Wesleyan Methodists position against the prevailing domination of the former planters and their Anglican religious leaders, appeals to the Home Office for additional finances to repair destroyed Wesleyan chapels which lay in ruins, and his insistence upon parity in race relations within the Jamaican Methodist Societies. The balancing act proved too difficult by 1834, and a Special District Meeting convened 14 May 1834 to discuss the implications of a physician's recommendation for Pennock to be removed to a milder climate for health reasons. I have to certify that from the long state of ill health, under which The Rev. Mr. Pennock has been suffering—the late severe illness of Mrs. Pennock, the recent distress of Mr. Pennock's family—and the protracted fever of his daughter . . . he should take the earliest opportunity of a change of climate–so as to resuscitate his own health and also that of his family.[33]

The "recent distress" to which the physician refers is the death of three of Pennock's children who died in succession.[34] The Special District Meeting was attended by Pennock, Isaac Whitehouse, John Corlett and David Kerr. This quorum authorized the Treasurer to "sell a bull at the amount of 150£ sterling . . . to pay for passage of the Chairman and his family to New York."[35] Pennock returned to Jamaica, in August of 1834, and would find it difficult to retain his previous post of Chairman of the Jamaica District. The minutes of a Special District Meeting, held 6th August 1834, record that Mr. John Corlett was Acting Chairman of the Jamaica District, whereupon Pennock's return was acknowledged with gratitude for the trip having restored his and his family's health.[36] The minutes also reflect the District Commit-

---

33. WMMS, *Missionary Correspondence*, Box 149, s.v. "Copy of Dr. Weir's Certificate."

34. Findlay, *Wesleyan Methodist Missionary Society*, 2:330.

35. WMMS, *Missionary Correspondence*, Box 149, s.v. "Minutes of a Special District Meeting."

36. Findlay, *Wesleyan Methodist Missionary Society*, 2:330. Findlay records that John

tee's authorization of Pennock's temporary assignment to Port Royal, until spring when he and his family intend to return to England.[37] Findlay writes that Pennock had resigned his position from New York, but upon returning to Jamaica was solicited by many of his colleagues to reassert rights to his former post.[38] After making the decision to remain in Jamaica, it quickly became clear to Pennock that Corlett was unwilling to vacate the position.

By early September, Pennock was growing irritated with Corlett's refusal to remove himself from the post of Acting Chairman.[39] This frustration would culminate in heated tension; this foreshadowed the acrimonious schism which would befall the Wesleyan Missionary Jamaica District. After several attempts requesting Corlett to return the District Books had gone unanswered, Pennock called the Synod together to reassert his office as Chairman of the District. Corlett and his faction refused to comply with Pennock's summons, and, on the 10th of September, 1834, the unheard of occurred: two separate Jamaica District Committee Meetings occurred, one at Wesley Chapel, Kingston with Thomas Pennock as Chairman and the other in Spanish Town, with John Corlett, as Acting Chairman.[40]

The British Conference of 1834 resolved the acrimony by assigning the Jamaica District Chairmanship to Rev. Valentine Ward, a universally respected Wesleyan Missionary, whose diplomatic style of leadership proved useful while he served as Chairman. So that there would be no confusion to the sweeping nature of his authority, the title, "Special Representative of the Missionary Committee and the Conference in the West Indies" was conferred upon him.[41] Unfortunately, his time in Jamaica was short-lived, as he fell ill and died within a year of his arrival to the island.[42] His tenure was

---

Corlett was Pennock's "frequent antagonist."

37. WMMS, *Missionary Correspondence*, Box 149, s.v. "Special Jamaica District Meeting."

38. Findlay, *Wesleyan Methodist Missionary Society*, 2:331.

39. Pennock documents in the minutes of the 10 September 1834 Special Jamaica District Meeting that he had written several letters to Corlett requesting that he return the District Books. Corlett only responded to one letter and never returned the District Books to Pennock.

40. WMMS, *Missionary Correspondence*, Box 149, s.v. "Synod Minutes (Corlett)," "Synod Minutes (Pennock)."

41. Findlay, *Wesleyan Methodist Missionary Society*, 2:331–32. The only missionary to hold this distinguished title prior to Ward was Thomas Coke.

42. Findlay, *Wesleyan Methodist Missionary Society*, 2:330. Ward fell seriously ill after a preaching engagement in Montego Bay and died on March 26, 1835. Findlay records the year of Ward's death as 1834, an obvious typographical error.

not long enough to resolve the tension surrounding racial prejudice that constantly undermined the harmony of the Jamaica District. Pennock's decision to remain in Jamaica, and advocate for colored persons to be entitled to full privileges of membership and opportunities within the Methodist Societies, increased his social isolation among his colleagues.

Methodist Advocate for Believer's Baptism

By 1837, Pennock was disillusioned and disenchanted with the social progress and spiritual state of the leaders of the Jamaica District. The fractious and frustrated state of Jamaican Wesleyan Methodism was merely a microcosm of the societal disarray which affected the island at large after emancipation. Pennock was constantly accused of "sowing disaffection" and was finally recalled to England in the spring of 1837 to explain his conduct.[43] Perhaps the persistent illness which he and his wife endured, the manner in which he was forced out of his role as Chairman of the Jamaica District, and the burial of all his children had soured his personality; upon his return to Jamaica, and weary of political conflict with his missionary colleagues, he decided to take up the offer made by several leading colored Methodists to secede and form a separate Methodist movement. Pennock's decision to leave the Wesleyan Methodist Missionary body was publicly announced in the Jamaican newspaper, *The Royal Gazette*, in a series of three letters. In his decision to resign from "Methodism As It Is," Pennock listed his objections to Methodism on the following grounds: *the Deed Poll, the Deeds of Trust, the novelty of the Theological Institution, Infant Baptism,* and the matter pertaining to the *Eternal Sonship of Jesus Christ*. For reasons of relevance to the socio-historical question this book is investigating, Pennock's explanation of his renunciation of infant baptism will be examined.

At the time of Pennock's resignation, all Wesleyan Missionaries faced a challenge as it pertained to the preferred mode of baptism, particularly among those who had been formerly enslaved. Popular Jamaican religiosity strongly identified with the rite of immersion because the majority of Jamaicans learned Christianity from black preachers and teachers, who had been initially converted by the black American preachers who traveled to Jamaica with the Loyalists during the Revolutionary period. Shirley C. Gordon claims that the Native Baptists were the "bedrock of all the slave

---

43. Findlay, *Wesleyan Methodist Missionary Society*, 2:332.

allegiance to Christianity."[44] This was evident by the overwhelming presence of slaves or former slaves who affiliated with Native Baptists.[45]

In *The Myth of the Negro Past*, anthropologist, Melville Herskovits, made the claim that the mode of baptism by immersion was one characteristic of African religiosity that was successfully retained in many Christian churches throughout the Americas. Herskovits has been taken to task for this claim, most notably by sociologist, E. Franklin Frazier, who insisted that the brutal conditions, which Africans faced in the New World, made it virtually impossible for African culture to survive, but that new forms of Afro-culture and religion had to be created.[46] Frazier conceded that various sociocultural factors, such as large African populations and absent European leadership within certain geographic regions of South America and the Caribbean, would allow for a stronger African cultural retention.[47]

Robert Stewart and Winston Lawson argue that the Baptists were most radical in their agitation against the plantocracy in the pre-emancipation period. The Baptist Church in Jamaica was and still is venerated because of its vigorous historical stance in the anti-slavery cause. Is it possible that Pennock's experience as a missionary in Jamaica during one of what could arguably be defined as its most turbulent period in history, may have caused him to reconsider his position on infant baptism? Clearly his Wesleyan Methodist Missionary colleagues faced the same baptismal dilemma, which seems to have intensified in the challenging years that the missionaries faced after emancipation. Pennock's nemesis, John Corlett submitted correspondence to the Mission Office which stated that he had to contend with the fixed belief that a Baptist baptism was best because "it washed away sins for good."[48]

---

44. Gordon, *God Almighty Make Me Free*, 41.

45. Gordon, *God Almighty Make Me Free*, 75. Gordon argues that the often repeated claim that free coloreds favored the Methodist society while the black slaves gravitated toward the Baptists is a generalization. She states that "accessibility rather than preference" was the ruling factor for most slaves who converted to Christianity in the years prior to Emancipation.

46. Herskovits published *The Myth of the Negro Past* in 1941. However, he established his groundbreaking claims in his PhD dissertation, *The Cattle Complex in East Africa*, published in 1923. E. Franklin Frazier refuted him with *The Negro Family in the United States*, published in 1939.

47. For the impact of absenteeism on the societal formation of Jamaica, see Patterson, *Sociology of Slavery*.

48. WMMS, *Missionary Correspondence*, Box 136, f. 556.

REBAPTISM CALMLY CONSIDERED

Other telling correspondence to the Mission Office comes from the Rev. John Edmondson Jr., who assumed the Jamaica District Chairmanship after the untimely death of Valentine Ward; his documentation reports that their dialogue with Baptists involved their claims that baptism by immersion was "necessary to salvation and that they [the Methodists] will be lost without it." Furthermore, they were often subjected to mockery and called, "basin of water Christians."[49] From the perspective of these two leading Wesleyan Missionaries, many Baptists in nineteenth-century Jamaica coupled the initiatory rite of believer's baptism to salvation itself. It could be argued that enslaved Native Baptists, such as Sam Sharpe, had existential reasons to identify their liberation from enslavement and oppression of believer's baptism sacramental ideology; but how did Thomas Pennock, a British citizen, who had been baptized as an infant as a Wesleyan Methodist, reach a strong conclusion in support of its doctrinal significance?

> The baptism of believing adults, is *solemnly* and *positively* enjoined by our Lord and Saviour Jesus Christ; but I cannot in the whole Word of God, find one clear and positive command for the baptism of *infants*. I am aware that . . . infant baptism derives considerable support from inferential and traditional arguments . . . and long existence and practice in the Christian Church. These arguments . . . do not, in my opinion give the ordinance a Divine sanction . . . do not make it either necessary or imperative. I believe that infants ought to be presented in the Church for God's blessing upon them . . . but I cannot see the necessity of applying to them the baptismal water, the application of which was, according to our Lord's commission to his Apostles and Ministers, designed to be a sign and seal of true repentance and faith.[50]

The Rev. David Kerr assumed the role of apologist for the Wesleyan Missionaries and he addressed all of Pennock's objections that were emphasized in, "*Methodism as it Is.*" Kerr reserves his response to Pennock's views on the subject of infant baptism for the refutation—he is incensed and does not mince words. Kerr asks Pennock to respond to three questions:

> Do you, Rev. Sir, deem it scripturally necessary to baptize at adult age, persons, who in their infancy received the Ordinance either from yourself, or any accredited Minister in the Gospel; and do you baptize them a *second* time?

---

49. WMMS, *Missionary Correspondence*, Box 139, f. 577
50. Pennock, "Rev. Pennock's Withdrawal From Methodism."

METHODIST MISSIONS AND BAPTIST RESISTANCE

> Do you think two baptisms better than one? And do you believe rebaptizing to be scriptural under the Christian system?
>
> Do you baptize infants "in the name of the Father, and of the Son, and of the Holy Ghost; and If you do so, do you not according to your own published principles, profane and even contemn The Sacred Name of the Deity, and the solemn Ordinance he has established in his Church?"[51]

Kerr goes on to state that Pennock's conduct is ungrateful and unfaithful to the Methodist Church, and "unhesitatingly affirms that Mr. P. is NOT a Methodist Preacher!"[52] He then begins his conclusion with a literal example in which Pennock publicly refused to baptize an infant, who was a child of a fellow Wesleyan Missionary at Parade Chapel, Sunday January 22nd, 1837; this demonstration of inconsistency (Pennock had baptized infants for 19 years as a Methodist minister) and impropriety was inexcusable for Kerr, and with a note of finality declared Pennock to be an enemy of the Church.[53]

The actual reasons for which Pennock refused to baptize the child of a fellow Wesleyan missionary are unclear, but what is clear is that among the most scathing charges Pennock submitted against his colleagues is that of the lack of evidence of holy living among the Methodists. "I am dissatisfied with 'Methodism' as it now is in Jamaica. . . . Conversions to God are but very seldom either witnessed or heard of, either in the Methodist Societies, or under the Methodist Ministry here. The Members of the Methodist Society here, are not, except in a few honorable instances, distinguished by *practical holiness of life*."[54] Pennock's critique continues to assert that the only two concerns that motivate the work of the Methodist society are the increase of membership and fundraising. "The superintendent preacher who has not, during the year, accomplished these two objects, is almost afraid to shew his face in the Annual District Meeting, at which . . . very little enquiry is made as to the *conversion of sinners* and the *sanctification*

---

51. Kerr, "An Answer to the Objections," 48. This document is extant in pamphlet form, and only two copies of it remain. Despite bibliographic information derived from the University of Edinburgh website, it is highly unlikely that *The Jamaica Watchman* would have published Kerr's document because its founder and editor, Edward Jourdan was a strong Pennock supporter. The document was printed in Kingston Jamaica, at the office of the *Royal Gazette*.
52. Kerr, "An Answer to the Objections," 49.
53. Kerr, "An Answer to the Objections," 50.
54. Pennock, "Rev. Pennock's Withdrawal From Methodism."

of believers, or into the causes which prevent the prosperity of the work of God in those two respects."[55] Pennock's charge accuses the most of the Jamaican Methodist leadership, of pursuing social respectability and financial security at the expense of providing effective ministry to the least privileged in Jamaican society. Pennock's use of the phrase, "the causes" could be interpreted to infer a direct relationship between his description of the poor state of affairs of Jamaican Methodism, and its perceived diminished relevance for the unreached masses of black humanity who had been formerly enslaved and were now dreadfully impoverished.

The sermons and writings of Thomas Pennock reveal a personality who was thoroughly convinced that the Wesleyan attributes of inward and outward holiness were bedrock principles of Christianity. His motivation for leaving the Wesleyan Methodist Missionary Society, and including infant baptism among his reasons for doing so, might be best attributed to his perception of the social value of a rite of Christian initiation for believing adults in an environment that was virulently hostile to Christians. Pennock's sermon to the apprentices, its admonition for them to display Christian conduct that could silence ignorant and ungodly men, could have easily been preached to the Anglican clergymen and Wesleyan Methodist leaders who succumbed to the pressures of societal *status quo* in matters of racial prejudice. Ted Campbell highlights a similar dilemma in the ministry of John Wesley. He states that Wesley's perspective of mission and ministry as a missionary of the Anglican Society for the Propagation of the Gospel (SPG) in 1736, was guided by a "radical recognition" that his own people, their society and their culture were not themselves Christian, and thus stood as much in need of the Gospel as any foreign people.[56] Therefore, Pennock seems to have concluded that infant baptism as practiced by the Church of England, and the Wesleyan Methodists was not only unscriptural, it denied baptismal candidates the opportunity to consciously mature into a position of repentance and faith. To make this point clear, Pennock urged his detractors, who would criticize his position on infant baptism, to take note of his adamant opposition to adult baptism without proper catechesis.[57]

---

55. Pennock, "Rev. Pennock's Withdrawal From Methodism."

56. Padgett, *Mission of the Church in Methodist Perspective*; Campbell, "John Wesley on the Mission of the Church," 54. The significance of Wesley's position is counter to most Evangelicals who readily claimed that Western Protestant Culture was Christian, and thus, categorically, all other cultures were inferior.

57. Pennock, "Rev. Pennock's Withdrawal From Methodism," 528.

METHODIST MISSIONS AND BAPTIST RESISTANCE

Reverend Thomas Pennock left his Grateful Hill circuit the 23rd of May 1837, and submitted his resignation to the Chairman of the Jamaica District by the 25th of June in 1837. This work argues that the religious and social environment of nineteenth-century Jamaica, provided a unique opportunity for Pennock (although encultured as a British Wesleyan Methodist to respect all human beings by their demonstrated capacity to contribute to established social order) to voluntarily become acculturated to the baptismal practice of another ecclesiastical culture, namely, the Jamaican Baptists who were most active in their vision of social transformation. Pennock suffered tremendously for his vigorous endorsement of racial egalitarianism, first, albeit in an indirect manner, through the lawless reign of terror and oppression from the mobs formed by the Anglican clergy who organized the Colonial Church Union; and secondly, from the direct experience of social isolation from his Wesleyan Methodist Missionary colleagues, for the sole reason of supporting the cause of complete personal and civic freedom for his capable black and colored sisters and brothers in the Jamaican Methodist societies. Thomas Pennock's rejection of infant baptism and sanction of believer's baptism could be viewed as his attempt to recreate meaning and power in the Methodism that he loved, but feared had been corrupted by irreligion exacerbated through racial prejudice.[58]

Pennock's movement immediately attracted about three hundred members from his former parish at Parade Chapel, and collected between £300-£400 toward a chapel and burial ground. Pennock rallied new members to support his separate Methodist movement by pledging to do three things: to "support the poor, bury the dead without charging fees, and to turn the financial management of the movement to colored stewards and leaders."[59] His theological anthropological understanding of freedom provided what was most vital to the real-life situations of potential converts among the formerly enslaved blacks and marginalized colored people: an acknowledgement of their humanity through communal efforts which exemplified their personal and civic freedom within his Independent Methodist Society. The result was the successful formation and nurture of several Independent Methodist societies in Jamaica.[60]

58. See Alexander, "Cultural Pragmatics."

59. Stewart, *Religion and Society*, 81.

60. In 1838, Pennock would align his movement with the schismatic Methodist group in England—the Wesleyan Association—led by Dr. Samuel Warren. In 1857, the Wesleyan Methodist Association would merge with the Wesleyan Reformers to form the United Methodist Free Churches. What is very interesting is that when Alfonso

REBAPTISM CALMLY CONSIDERED

The process of dismantling the "sugar plantocracy" resulted in a contestation of power, which emerged between races, social strata, political factions and denominational affiliation in early and mid-nineteenth-century Jamaica. Consequently, blacks, colored persons and whites, experienced relative degrees of freedom in their environment. Patterson's argument that the high valuation of freedom is implicit in the diminished social status of one's person, can be used to support the claim that Thomas Pennock's tenuous social position uniquely positioned him to adopt a definition of freedom consistent with John Wesley's theological anthropology—that all persons ought have the opportunity to attain spiritual, physical and intellectual liberation through Christ.

Ritual, Resistance, and Personhood

During the period of legal enslavement, even though most free colored persons advocated for emancipation, as they appealed for the attainment of their civil rights, it was not uncommon for them to hold attitudes of superiority toward blacks due to their enhanced social status. Free blacks in search of social mobility were much more likely to join the Methodist church versus the enslaved blacks, so the result was a broad racial mixture for the Methodist Societies in Jamaica and throughout the Caribbean. Methodists could boast that their membership comprised of whites and blacks, but most prominently it was the free colored population who readily identified with the evangelical message and the emphasis on morality and education. This was largely in part to the relationship between class and color in the West Indies. "A large part of the Methodist membership in the 1830s consisted of colored small proprietors who were the masters of apprentices."[61] When Methodist missionaries arrived to the colonies, they often had to make the difficult choice of who they would direct their missionary activities toward. W. G. Barrett arrived to Jamaica in the 1830s and learned that he would have to choose who to work with in order gain confidence of the growing and influential freed colored population. "He

---

Dumar, the founder of the A.M.E. Church in Jamaica, extended an offer to churches to join the A.M.E. Church, he received extraordinary response and support from many existing United Methodist Free Churches in Jamaica and brought several into the A.M.E. connectional church. See Beckerlegge, *United Methodist Free Churches*, 28. Also, A.M.E. *Missionary Correspondence*, Box 41, s.v. Dumar Folder.

61. Stewart, *Religion and Society*, 71.

METHODIST MISSIONS AND BAPTIST RESISTANCE

deliberately chose to emphasize his work among the 'brown' students in his school . . . [Methodist] missionaries made their preferential choices for brown skin in the light of their perception of the structure and conflicts of Jamaican society."[62]

The liberation theologian, James Cone argued that the spiritual problems of the wealthy or financially secure are not the same kinds of problems that the poor encounter as it relates to matters of theology. As it relates to matters of theology, people with financial security have philosophical problems of non-belief, i.e., *"What should I believe?"* Conversely, people who are financially impoverished within a materialistic culture have an anthropological problem as it relates to faith, that of a non-person, i.e., *"Who should I become?"*[63] Englebert Mveng's theory of anthropological poverty assists in understanding the depth of the trauma of European enslavement on the psyche and body of the African person who has been enslaved. After emancipation, most former Jamaican slaves became disillusioned when social dignity, political access, economic opportunity, and racial equality continued to elude them. Malidoma Patrice Somé argues that within African spirituality ritual is the mechanism which uproots the source of dysfunctional affairs as it relates to a human's state of being in the world.[64] It is from the world of the spirit that ritual derives the power to intervene in human affairs and influence (for good or ill) the vitality of human existence.

Intervention in human affairs from the spirit world cannot occur with some form of transition ritual. In the West generally, and within Christianity particularly, rituals which mark transitions within the human life cycle have undergone radical change in the last century. The Roman Catholic Church developed rich sacramental rites to celebrate birth, confirmation, marriage, forgiveness, reconciliation, sickness and death among the faithful. The sweeping changes that occurred during the Protestant Reformation in Europe unintentionally ushered in the period of Enlightenment whose sterile emphasis on reason essentially pauperized the vitality of ritual in the West. For instance, the contemporary Western postmodern world and even its antecedent, the modern world, offer negligible replacements for the adolescent puberty initiation rite within pre-modern societies.[65] For

---

62. Stewart, *Religion and Society*, 72–73.
63. Cone, *For My People*, 97.
64. Somé, *Ritual*, 25.
65. Grimes, *Deeply Into the Bone*, 117. Grimes argues that a ritual does not have to be *called* initiation in order to *be* initiation. He suggests that one ought to look for initiation

pre-modern communities, the ritual of the initiation rite is one of existential importance for the individual and, by extension, the tribe. It is the seminal event when one ultimately consents to embrace death in order to be reborn as *another*. It is my argument that the Native Baptist worldview with its emphasis upon believer's baptism by conversion, structured the baptismal ritual to mimic the initiation rite within communities that practice African traditional religion. Native Baptist congregants essentially recreated the initiation rite in an act of resistance against the dominant ecclesial and social order to reorient and rehumanize themselves within a system that intentionally dehumanized their personhood and erased their positive contributions to society. While rituals acknowledge the normal stages of human development, a rite of passage becomes necessary to assist humans navigate the treacherous places of human existence. "A rite of passage is a set of symbol-laden actions by means of which one passes through a dangerous zone, negotiating it safely and memorably . . . to enact a rite of passage is also to transform."[66] When human beings attempt to negotiate the treacherous path of human tragedy without acknowledging it through some form of ritual, self-alienation occurs.[67] The leaders and members of the Native Baptist community were the most deprived of social, economic, and political standing within Jamaican society. They had been rendered the status of the non-person. The pattern of Christian initiation within the Native Baptist system became a rite of passage for its oppressed and often distressed membership, and the rite became recognized for its efficacy, even for many outside their communities of faith.[68] The rite of passage in-

---

under other names: orientation, promotion, conversion, confirmation, and ordination. While these occasions indicate the beginning of a process of advancement, one could argue that the complexity of Western postmodern life often creates such an alienation of the self that it damages the efficacy of ritual. Jeffrey Alexander's theory of Cultural Pragmatics confronts the concern of ritual inadequacy by developing a macro-sociological model of social action that he calls *cultural performance*. See Alexander, "Cultural Pragmatics," 529.

66. Grimes, *Deeply Into the Bone*, 117.

67. Cooper, *Sin, Pride & Self-Acceptance*, 103. Cooper argues self-alienation occurs when the actual self, which consists of real feelings and experience, becomes twisted, distorted, and stretched into a mold called the "appropriate" self. This censorship activity has the end result of self-estrangement and ignorance of our real needs, desires, and dispositions toward life.

68. Gordon, *God Almighty Make Me Free*, 116. Gordon writes: "The practice of total immersion at baptism and the largely attended ceremonies at the river and seasides seemed to many Jamaicans a much more convincing admission to Christian membership than a chapel baptism."

METHODIST MISSIONS AND BAPTIST RESISTANCE

corporated symbolic language, actions, and objects, which signified deep meaning within the hierarchical context of Jamaican society and re-echoed the significance that the rite of baptism possessed within the early church.

Enslaved Africans in Jamaica endured a state of persecution which mimicked the era of persecution in the early Church. The system of enslavement was one which encapsulated the entire society of the island. All social relationships were defined and affected by it—it was a psychological, emotional, political and economic reality. Enslaved persons who converted to Christianity under Liele's ministry in Jamaica were attracted to the teleological possibilities within the faith. They anticipated emancipation and living in a space outside the hellish realm of the slave system, life after death.[69] For those who decided to conform their lifestyle to the moral mandates, the salvific work of Christ was enthusiastically embraced by slaves. Conversion and consenting to baptism was a means for many to acquire confidence that one's sins were forgiven and that heaven would be their portion. Overwhelmingly, the preaching services which prompted the convert to consent to a reorienting of his or her life was precipitated by charismatic, affective, and revivalist content. However, the conversion motif could not be defined as a manner in which one would be considered coerced, or brainwashed, into joining the Christian band. Social psychology acknowledges the persuasive dynamic of crowds that are emotionally aroused as a "social pressure" loaded with intense joy, guilt, or fear, such that individuals are compelled to respond. However, these feelings, when not undergirded with intellectual and affective content, would not typically bear out under the rigors of catechesis prior to the actual moment of baptism. Conversion motifs among the slaves certainly varied; however, a baptismal candidate's preparation for the rite was intensely personal, largely mystical and that was directly connected to the Afro-Baptist cosmos which Liele and his ministerial colleagues transmitted which supported the metaphysical phenomena of visions and dreams as adequate proof of conversion and readiness for baptism.

69. Conversion narratives of the slaves in Jamaica were often recorded to reflect their desire for blissful life after death. There is little to no documentation that the conversion experience conveys the idea that liberty is an expectation for slaves, which is an interesting departure from themes of liberty within the Early Methodist conversion narratives described by D. Bruce Hindmarsh. No doubt this is due to the coded language that the slaves were forced to speak when talking to missionaries about their faith. Sam Sharpe's appropriation of the themes of liberty can be viewed as an indication of how the earliest converts to Christianity imbibed the hope of emancipation from sin and slavery. See Hindmarsh, "'My Chains Fell Off, My Heart Was Free,'" 910–29.

REBAPTISM CALMLY CONSIDERED

Preparation for Immersion

The fieldwork of Herskovits and Herskovits in the Caribbean is helpful for describing the process of preparing for the ritual of baptism for persons who hold to an Afro-Baptist cosmology, as was prevalent in the Ethiopian Baptist Church.

> When a man or woman comes to the teacher with his vision or dream, and offers himself as a candidate for baptism, he undergoes a period of instruction that some say last for three months, others three weeks, a month, or loner, depending on the candidate. . . . The eyes of the candidates are bound . . . the river, or the spot on the sea-shore where the baptizing—which must always take place in "living water"—is to be carried out. . . . Each candidate, holding a lighted candle, is immersed three times. (Note: "Any river is the Jordan"—the river in Palestine where Jesus Christ was baptized by John the Baptist.)[70]

Similarly, the following is a description of training for baptismal candidates with a quote from the minister as he instructed them for the ritual.

> Baptism is a death: you are leaving the world of men and entering the world of God. For this baptism, this death, you will be buried in the watery tomb which is Jordan. After the death, you will be resurrected and will join the ranks of everlasting life through Jesus. . . . You are on a spiritual journey through the valley of the shadow of death.[71]

In one of his earliest letters to the London Missionary Society, Liele writes, "The people at first persecuted us, both at meetings and baptisms, but God be praised, they seldom bother us now."[72] The early conversion experiences of any persecuted or despised minority, dictate that the symbolic act of initiation is the most salient. Stephen Glazier uses the anthropological work of Edward Sapir to highlight the importance for social scientists and historians to examine the socio-political factors which contribute to the "authenticity and genuineness" of ritual within Afro-Caribbean religions.[73] Glazier argues that "with respect to Caribbean religions, the religions of the

---

70. Herskovits, *Trinidad Village*, 199–203.
71. McCollin-Moore, "Anglican Meets Spiritual Baptist," 66.
72. Liele et al., "Letters Showing the Rise and Progress," 71.
73. Glazier, "New World African Ritual," 421.

white planter class were by definition spurious, while the religions created by the slaves were of necessity genuine, in Sapir's sense of the terms."[74]

The socio-historical potency of the baptismal ritual of immersion may be found in the connection between the Judeo-Christian notion of covenant and the African-Jamaican spiritual inheritance of oath-taking. "Total immersion closely resembled African water rites. Blacks 'were responding to this ritual as an initiation rite . . . that the Methodists could not provide.'"[75] To press the comparative model of spurious and genuine ritual further, infant baptism was solidly identified as the ritual of the Anglican Church, the religion of the enslaver and the oppressor. Rev. George Wilson Bridges, the Anglican rector at St. Ann's Bay on the north side of the island, has historically been the representation of terror and irreligion against slaves (and the missionaries who desired to evangelize them) within the Anglican Church. Bridges published an article in 1823 against William Wilberforce, which emphasized the benevolence of the slave society in the West Indies. A critique of the article in the *Christian Observer* lists some of his observations as follows: "Want is unknown to the slaves in these isles; while the toils of the British laborer, the sweat of whose care worn brow, has hardly gained a scanty substance for his craving children."[76] Bridges was a vocal proponent of the ideology that humanity existed in gradations along a vertical scale in which whites were at the top, while blacks were at the bottom, "where the gap to the highest of the animals, the orangutan, is not very great."[77] His frequent publications consistently articulated the ideology of racial superiority of whites and bestiality of blacks. The cruelty in which he treated his slaves was displayed and used as a tool for the abolitionists to advance the cause of emancipation. The *Anti-Slavery Monthly Reporter* published the most sensational episodes of his terror toward one of his slaves, Kitty Hylton. In the episode, Bridges mercilessly beats and kicks Hylton, his domestic helper, before having her flogged to the point

---

74. Glazier, "New World African Ritual," 422.

75. Pitts, *Old Ship of Zion*, 45.

76. "Rev. G.W. Bridges on the Effects of Manumission," 760.

77. Curtin, *Two Jamaicas*, 41. See Bridges, *Annals of Slavery*. In 1829, the Court of Kings Bench rendered a judgment of libel against Bridges for printing a false accusation that two free men of color had attempted to murder white men, which resulted in their deportation to St. Domingo. The men returned to Jamaica, sued Bridges for slander, and won the case. See "Court of King's Bench," 823. The *Annals of Slavery* was forbidden to be published again. Bridges hatred for free blacks and coloreds drew the ire of Wesleyan Methodists because many of his targets were members of the Methodist Societies.

of death, all for having killed the wrong turkey for dinner.[78] Interestingly enough, Bridges is attributed to have written extraordinary claims about baptizing thousands of slaves within his parish. "During my residence in the parish . . . I have actually baptized 9,413 slaves." His critics assail this claim by retorting,

> If they were not converted to Christianity, or if they did not understand the nature of the solemn vow and covenant they were called to make, what a perfect mockery of religion, what a prostitution of a sacred initiatory rite of baptism is here made be the subject of this minister's boast! When he sprinkled them with water "in the name of the Father, and of the Son, and of the Holy Ghost" and received them into the congregation of Christ's flock . . . [was he not conscious] that respect for all his Neophytes, that these were words without a meaning?[79]

The meaning ascribed to the ritual of immersion empowered it to become the single most important element for the provision of religious identity or membership in the Native Baptist church. The meaning of the ritual was depicted early in a letter from Liele, dated in 1791, which insisted that Methodists be rebaptized before becoming members of the congregation. Liele writes, "A few of Mr. Wesley's people, after immersion, join us and continue with us."[80] An 1802 Baptist missionary publication recorded their activities of Liele's church.

> They preach every Lord's day from 10 to 12 o'clock in the morning, and from 4 to 6 in the evening; and on Tuesday and Thursday evening, from seven to eight. They administer the Lord's Supper every month, and baptize once in three months. The members are divided into smaller classes which meet separately every Monday evening, to be examined respecting their daily walk and conversation.[81]

Those devoted persons, who were among the first converts of Liele's Ethiopian Baptist Church, made the counter-cultural decision to adopt a new spiritual identity through the cleansing power of water in baptism by

---

78. "Rev. G.W. Bridges, and his Slave Kitty Hylton," 373. This account was also published in full by Henry Bleby. See Bleby, 83–87.
79. Bridges, "Rev. G.W. Bridges on the Effects of Manumission," 762.
80. Liele et al., "Letters Showing the Rise and Progress," 2.
81. Rusling, "Note on Early Negro Baptist History," 365.

METHODIST MISSIONS AND BAPTIST RESISTANCE

immersion for the hope of peace and joy beyond the traumas of life in slave society.

However, for others the moral expectations were too excessive, and some Native Baptist leaders of Independent Black churches would make allowances for the social realities that permeated the lives of blacks in nineteenth-century Jamaica. These allowances included an expectation of healing, joy, and peace in this life, which aspects of African culture could and did affirm. As many of the leaders and members of the Anglican Church perpetuated brutal antagonism against blacks and coloreds, and Wesleyan Methodists wrestled with indecision of racial equality, Liele's ritual of immersion evolved into a Native Baptist rite of passage, and provided a marked distinction between "spurious and genuine" religion. Liele's covenant provided the enslaved community with a framework from which their independent congregations would derive harmony and integration with African-Jamaican religiosity. These persons assented to the primary elements of Liele's doctrine along with the cleansing ritual of baptism, and the hope of eternal bliss beyond the grave; however, they found it necessary to cling to some of the religio-cultural practices that sustained their embattled community along with the social tactics of survival that the system of slavery taught them. During their worship services, symbols and ritualization were employed that reflected a ritual knowledge, which Western Protestant Christianity would fail to recognize and lack the ability to interpret and therefore control the ritual meaning.[82] As it pertained to the baptismal ritual, the set of symbols that constituted a valid baptism remained relatively consistent. All that was typically required for baptism to take place was a pool of water; a wooden cross, a candle, and a minister that the community recognized as qualified to properly administer the baptismal vows.[83] This vow has witnesses that are not just the human beings

---

82. Symbolism within Jamaican Native Baptist churches varied tremendously according to the degree of influence of either *Zion* or *Pukkimina*, the two major groups which emerged out of the late nineteenth-century Revivalist movement. See Seaga, "Revival Cults in Jamaica."

83. While performing my field research in 2010, a young Jamaican teenager who was an active leader in the Young People's Department of the A.M.E. Church expressed her astonishment that a popular practice in early Jamaican A.M.E. baptismal ritual—called "the vow"—was not in the baptismal liturgy of the A.M.E. Hymnal. "The vow" portion of the baptismal ceremony occurs when the minister queries the baptismal candidate on his or her sincerity and commitment to Christianity and the moral lifestyle that would be expected of him or her as members of the Church. The candidate responds to the query by taking a public vow and declares to commit his or her life to Christ, "until the

that are participating in the ceremony; the Triune God, angelic spirits, and even nature can be called upon to give an account of the persons having sweared to follow Christ.[84]

The culturally unique element of the vow shaped the language and symbolism of the entire rite. A wooden cross could be used as a symbol of Christ's sacrifice, or as tactile instrument by which one actually picked up the cross in an embodiment of ritual action to publicly commit to live a sacrificial life in devotion to God's Christ. A candle could be used as a visual aid to symbolize the illuminating life of moral excellence and virtue role that each new member of the Church is to exemplify. These symbols (and others) provided sociological cues and enhanced communal solidarity, which shaped the importance of the ritual for the Native Baptist communities of faith and ensured the preservation of their fundamental Christian values. For anthropologically impoverished persons, immersion was a rite of passage that communicated new identity through symbolic power. Persons stripped of the knowledge of cultural ties of blood and soil, like Sam Sharpe were able to extrapolate the meaning of liberty through the acquisition of a Christian identity which would insist upon the emancipation of their bodies, so as to mirror the refreshment of their liberated souls.

---

day of judgment." This element of the ritual is performed without the aid of the rubric in the A.M.E. Hymnal—an indication of its place as a unique element within popular African-Jamaican religiosity, which has been syncretized with Western European Protestant Christianity—in a twenty-first-century form of African Methodism.

84. Ministers in the Jamaican A.M.E. Church of the early and mid-twentieth century frequently pointed out the presence of natural phenomena in the sight of the baptismal candidates and the congregation as "witnesses" to the public commitment to Christianity by the baptizands, especially during a baptism in the river or sea. Hence, the nature itself, "the trees, stars, birds, or the rocks" could be called upon to remind the baptizands of their commitment to the Christian faith. I am indebted to my father and many personal interviewees of older members of the Jamaican A.M.E. Church for sharing their experience of this form of liturgical expression and (African) spirituality.

Chapter Five

THE ALLEN-WESLEYAN LEGACY IN JAMAICA

THIS CHAPTER SEEKS TO trace the missionary activity of the A.M.E. Church as it relates to the missionary assignment of the Rev. Alfonso Dumar, the North American clergyman tasked with organizing the fledging Jamaican mission into a conference of self-sustaining churches. Dumar assumed his work with a zealous commitment to introduce and expand the legacy of Allen and the tenets of African Methodism into Jamaica. However, he underestimated the socio-cultural dynamic that operated within the historical context of Jamaica, which would make a full assent to the Wesleyan commitment to infant baptism problematic. This author argues that Dumar's insistence upon infant baptism resulted in the *unintended consequence of an additional water ritual for infants* within the early A.M.E. Church of Jamaica identified as 'christening.' This ritual whereupon a newborn was sprinkled with water, was not deemed a proper substitute for an individual's public confession of faith and believer's baptism by immersion—the recognized Christian initiation ritual for adherents of popular Jamaican religiosity. Alfonso Dumar's missionary activity undoubtedly shaped the manner in which the continuous liturgical usage of water was demonstrated within the A.M.E. Church of Jamaica during its formative years, until the present day.

The African Methodist Episcopal Church has been officially involved in overseas missions since its missionary work in Haiti commenced in 1823. As early as 1849, the A.M.E. Church aspired to extend its presence from North America to the African continent and the West Indies. The Baltimore Annual Conference adopted a resolution in 1849 which authorized the church to establish missions in these geographical locations. Bishop

REBAPTISM CALMLY CONSIDERED

C.S. Smith, who served as A.M.E. Historiographer writes, "The purpose of the resolution, however, did not materialize. This was caused by the desire to do being mistaken for the ability to perform."[1] Missionary activity in the Caribbean expanded decades later, through the outreach of the British Methodist Episcopal Church (BME).[2] However, it was the vision and missionary zeal of Bishop Henry McNeal Turner that forced the A.M.E. church out of complacency and into a committed, funded effort which supported missionaries in foreign fields to organize A.M.E. churches.

Turner was instrumental in the founding of the Home and Foreign Mission Department in 1864, as the A.M.E. church sought to gain new ground in the South after the Civil War. Stephen Angell argues that "Turner was a chief instigator of the most momentous transformation that has occurred in A.M.E. Church history, the mission to the South. . . . When he joined the A.M.E. Church in 1858, it had about 20,000 members, and less than four decades later in 1896, it numbered 452,725."[3] Turner's tireless efforts in the South resulted in him virtually single-handedly organizing the entire state of Georgia. At the turn of the century, Turner's sights turned to Africa. By the mid-1870s Turner could discern that the federal government commitment to Reconstruction was waning. Republican state governments were losing power in the South and the presence of federal troops was slim. Turner began to actively initiate dialogue with the American Colonization Society, submitting an article for their journal in 1875. "There is no more doubt in my mind that we have ultimately to return to Africa than there is

---

1. Smith, *History of African Methodist Episcopal Church*, 20.

2. The British Methodist Episcopal Church (BME) was formed as an offshoot of the A.M.E. Church in response to the adoption of a motion by the Reverend Benjamin Stewart of Chatham, Ontario, at the Philadelphia Annual Conference of 1856. The harsh restrictions imposed upon freed blacks after the Congressional passage of the Fugitive Slave Act in 1850 sent tremors through the predominantly northern based denomination, such that ministers who had been former slaves and 'migrated' to Canada were afraid of travelling to conferences in the United States. Reverend Stewart suggested that the established A.M.E. Churches in Canada form a separate church. The new church was called the British Methodist Church as a way of designating complete separation from the United States and, by extension, freedom from the conditions of enslavement. Bishop Smith writes that the BME started a mission in the Danish West Indies and British Guiana in 1873 under Bishop Nazrey. The A.M.E. Church would assume responsibility for these missions when the BME Church re-obligated its leadership and congregations to the A.M.E. Church in 1881 under Bishop Disney.

3. Angell, *Bishop Henry McNeal*, 3.

of the existence of a God; and the sooner we begin to recognize the fact and prepare for it, the better it will be for us as a people."[4]

The presidential election of 1876 conferred the honor upon Rutherford Hayes, the Republican candidate, but Turner was cautiously optimistic. His political clout gained his a meeting with the newly elected president who relayed to Turner his benevolent intentions toward those recently freed from enslavement. Turner understood that political concessions had to be made to the Democratic Party to appease their wrath and mitigate the vindictiveness that would cause outbreaks of racial violence in the South. However, but the "Compromise of 1877" instituted by President Hayes was perceived by Turner and southern blacks to be tantamount to outright betrayal and cruelty. A Southern Democrat was appointed to the presidential cabinet, the Republican Party lost control of southern state governments as a result of patronage given to the Democratic Party by Hayes, and the last straw— the removal of federal troops from the South. Having grown depressed and weary from political betrayal and the racial hatred and injustice blacks had to endure—Turner cast his lot in with the A.M.E. Church and the African emigration movement. His bitterness is evident in his response as he was interviewed during the presidential election of 1880,

> I am down upon the whole *nation*. I think my race has been treated with the kindness that a hungry snake treats a helpless frog . . . while studying the Negro, I have been made sick a thousand times—wished I had never been born, so that I might not have been a witness to the deviltry perpetrated upon my people by a so-called civilized country.[5]

Turner's missionary endeavor on the African continent began with his initial voyage to Africa, arriving in Sierra Leone in November 1891; and resulted in the organization of four annual conferences in Africa, one in Liberia, one in Pretoria, Transvaal, Sierra Leone, and Queenstown, S. Africa. Gayraud Wilmour has stated that "Turner's visit to Africa was a strategic contribution to the revival of missionary emigrationism within the A.M.E. Church."[6]

In order to gain support for these new missions, Turner initiated, produced and served as editor of the *Voice of Missions,* an A.M.E. publication intended to disseminate information to A.M.E. membership regarding the

4. Turner, "Letter to The American Colonization Society," 42.
5. Turner, *Christian Recorder*; Redkey, *African Repository*, 49. Emphasis added.
6. Wilmour, *Black Radicalism*, 215.

growing missionary efforts of the Church.[7] In January 1893, the first issue of the newspaper was released. On the first page were the minutes of the previous Missionary Board meeting held on November 18, 1892; so that subscribers would have an indication of the missions that the A.M.E. Home and Foreign Department of Missions already sponsored.

> The board decided that in view of assistance already given to the mission at Port-Au-Prince, Republic of Hayti, W.I. that the mission be henceforth classed as a Station in the Twelfth Episcopal District, providing that the presiding bishop shall first satisfy himself and the secretary of missions that such action is advisable.[8]

This statement designating the transfer of responsibility of the Haiti mission to the Twelfth (12th) Episcopal District, draws attention to a problem of instability that would continue to plague the Caribbean region. The responsibility for the mission conferences in the West Indies would be frequently be parsed out to varying Episcopal Districts.[9] Nevertheless, the minutes conclude with resolutions from Dr. W. B. Derrick, the Secretary of Missions:

> Whereas we have listened with great delight, likewise with great profit to the very able and encouraging address delivered by the Rt. Rev. H. M. Turner . . . the pioneer bishop in foreign lands, in said address has given flood of light thereby opening new and effectual doors, in and through which, as a church, we may enter more successfully upon the work which African Methodism is commissioned to perform beyond the seas, and whereas the many wise, practiceable and feasible plans suggested by him is a striking evidence of the fact that he has entered mind, heart and soul into the great work which the church has committed to him.[10]

When the first issue of the *Voice of Missions* was published, the Home and Foreign Missionary Society of the A.M.E. Church divided its work in

---

7. Angell concludes that the primary goal of the journal was to generate interest and disseminate information pertaining to Turner's Back-to-Africa emigrationist vision. In my estimation, Turner's missionary zeal is rooted in his passion as an evangelist, and his concern for the state of African-Americans in the USA, to that end, he supported the A.M.E. Church's missionary activity in Mexico as well.

8. "Minutes of the Home and Foreign Missionary Society," 1.

9. In 1904, the General Conference assigned the West Indies to the Third District, in 1916, the West Indies were in the Fifteenth District, and in 1920, the West Indies were a part of the Eighteenth District.

10. "Minutes of the Home and Foreign Missionary Society," 1.

THE ALLEN-WESLEYAN LEGACY IN JAMAICA

the foreign field into three areas: the West Indies (Haiti, St. Domingo, and St. Thomas, Danish, WI), the African missions of Liberia and Sierra Leone, and the Indian Territory in North America. Derrick's resolution may appear to be superfluous, but the work of Turner inspired many to dedicate themselves to the missionary effort. Among those inspired was the Rev. Alfonso Dumar, an ambitious, charismatic man who had been educated at Wilberforce—the citadel of A.M.E. institutions of higher education. His inspiration and call to mission would lead him to organize the A.M.E. Church in Jamaica.

The early twentieth century in which Dumar worked as a missionary in Jamaica was one in which the world engaged in unprecedented transnational encounter. Ideas and theories about nationalism, imperialism, peoplehood, independence, and visions of collective destiny interpreted the manner in which these international encounters were interpreted. For African-Americans, the bitter failure of Reconstruction formed the context of their existential circumstance. The experience of being a formerly enslaved people currently subjugated and colonized in the South, provided cultural self-understanding that was often currency in dialogue with other colonized persons of colour around the world. African Methodist missionaries were therefore, very vocal opponents to the racism and violence that often accompanied European colonial expansion, which ran the risk of an antagonistic relationship with colonial governments. "The role of the A.M.E. Church in South Africa after 1896 and the northward spread of its work into central Africa, aroused fears and anxiety that African-Americans were likely to stir up racial unrest."[11]

The West Indies and by extension, the Caribbean region at large, would pose unique challenges to the A.M.E. Church missionary department. The Caribbean islands are physically separated, and the variety and complexity of historical colonialism and its relationship with African traditions create a striking amalgam of linguistic, religious, dietary, social, literary and artistic current that result in the uniquely rich and diverse Caribbean culture. Any successful missionary effort in the Caribbean foreign field must possess perceptive ability which understands and is not intimidated by the complex historical, political, economic, socio-cultural, and spiritual factors at the root of its cohesive and divisive nature. When Dumar initially arrived to Jamaica in 1912, the United States was hungry for additional markets. The USA's astounding economic growth had been accompanied

---

11. Killingray, "Black Atlantic Missionary Movement," 20.

by an equally astounding series of economic downturns. "Nearly half the years between the 1870s and World War I were depression . . . 1873–1879, 1882–85, 1893–97, 1907–8, and 1913–1915. . . . In this context, social and economic remedies were at a premium; indeed, this was a time of frenetic activity in inventing, proposing, and debating solutions of all sorts."[12] The USA's desire for additional markets generated profound interest in Latin America and the Caribbean, which President Teddy Roosevelt articulated best with military intervention.[13]

Poor Jamaicans responded to the colonial overreach of the United States and its accompanying political and economic uncertainty in the Caribbean, in predominately three ways, migration, socialism and religious expression. Jamaicans migrated to England, Panama and the United States in massive numbers to improve the economic hardship they faced at home. Many Jamaican intellectuals who travelled abroad would make vital contributions to the Harlem Renaissance, the Socialist effort and the Pan-African movement. Those who stayed often interpreted their dilemma of socio-economic impoverishment through the Revivalism or Christian Myalism that informed the doctrine and praxis of Jamaican popular religiosity.

It is this chapter's premise that Dumar arrived to conduct mission work in Jamaica with a cultural worldview that was informed by an ethnic consciousness informed by Richard Allen's legacy of Wesleyan doctrine and social protest, and well within the cultural milieu of Reverdy Ransom's Black Social Gospel.[14] Both necessarily predated Alain Locke's *New Negro* movement and Woodrow Wilson's '*self-determination*.' Lamen Sanneh develops an argument in *Translating the Message* which confronts the

---

12. Jacobson, *Barbarian Virtues*, 18.

13. Jacobson, *Barbarian Virtues*, 40, 41. Between 1898 and 1920, Roosevelt deployed US marines to the Caribbean twenty times to restore order, or establish stability on terms dictated by the United States. "When asked what exactly would constitute stability in Cuba, General Leonard Wood replied, 'When money can be borrowed at a reasonable rate of interest and when capital is willing to invest in the island, a condition of stability will have been reached.'" The Spanish-Cuban-American War was transformative in the venue of Latin American trade, during the conflict, the US eliminated Spain's presence and assumed control of their Cuban and Puerto Rican colonies.

14. Scholars such as Gary Dorrien, Terrell Dale Goddard, Cornelius Bynum and Calvin Morris have introduced scholarship that recognizes a distinction between the era of the Social Gospel and the synthesis of black activism and the Progressive Movement at the turn of the twentieth century. Dorrien uses the term Black Social Gospel that exists with four identifiable strands of praxis by the most visible and vocal black leaders in the United States at the time.

THE ALLEN-WESLEYAN LEGACY IN JAMAICA

assumption that Western missionary activity among indigenous peoples outside Western culture must necessarily parallel colonialism. He proposes that Christianity at its root—is an exercise in translation.

> Christianity, from its origins identified itself with the need to translate out of Aramaic and Hebrew, and from that position came to exert a dual force in its historic development. . . . [Thus] two subjects, the Judaic and the Gentile, became closely intertwined in the Christian dispensation, both crucial to the formative image of the new religion.[15]

While the island of Jamaica is a part of the Americas, and hence 'inside' Western culture, the highly influential African component of its cultural heritage offers a particular challenge to any missionary from North America. Sanneh's argument concludes that vernacular translation can have an impact of renewal on ethnic consciousness, and need not compromise the cultural self-understanding of the convert. Translation in the broadest use of the term necessarily implies the porosity of culture. In contrast to Sanneh's example of the missionary translation of the Bible, for African Methodists it occurred through the message of racial egalitarianism which identified with the struggle against European colonialism. The particular occasion of Alfonso Dumar's organization of the A.M.E. Church in Jamaica would be peppered with vestiges of paternalism, and dimensions of cultural opacity which often surfaced because of the continuing presence of Revivalism in many of the A.M.E. churches.

The Arrival of Alfonso Dumar

Dumar possessed charisma and drive which garnered positive attention from the Rev. R. R. Wright Jr. a General Officer who wielded considerable influence in the early twentieth-century A.M.E. Church.[16] There is

---

15. Sanneh, *Translating the Message*, 1.

16. R. R.Wright Jr. was one of the first blacks to earn a PhD from the University of Pennsylvania. He served the church as a General Officer and was elected a bishop in 1936. His father, R. R. Wright Sr., gained notoriety as a young boy for an event that transpired after the Civil War ended. His mother sent him to a school for former slaves even though it was hundreds of miles away from home. It was at this school that he had an exchange that inspired a once famous poem by John Greenleaf Whittier. When his class was asked by retired Union general what message he should take back to the Northerners who fought for their freedom, Wright Sr. spoke up: "Sir, tell them we are rising." Wright Sr. would rise to the rank of Major in the US Army, serve as principal of Georgia State

handwritten communication which depicts Wright's referral of Dumar to J.W. Rankin, the man elected to the post of Secretary of Mission at the 1912 General Conference.[17] Although the A.M.E. Church had established a slight missionary presence, it lacked continuous oversight and organization.[18] Dumar's correspondence to Rankin and his frequent submissions to the prominent Kingston newspaper, the *Jamaica Gleaner* reflect a strong, confident personality who was particularly skilled in the arena of public relations. These attributes would serve him well, as the number of North American based denominations staking their claim to win Jamaican souls for Christ during the early twentieth century were numerous. Other relative newcomers were The Salvation Army which arrived in 1887, and the Seventh Day Adventists, which arrived the same year as the A.M.E. Church. Dumar made an initial trip to Jamaica in 1912, and relocated to the island in 1914. When he made the formal application to register the A.M.E. Church as an official denomination with the government of Jamaica, he described himself in this manner:

> Your excellency:
> As per the recent Act "The Alien Missionary and Educational Work Law": I am making this my application for your permission to continue my work as a Christian Minister of the African Methodist Episcopal Church. I am a citizen of Bath, Maine, United States of America, and started my ministerial labour in Kingston, October 1914, and have erected Allen Temple A.M.E. Church, 89 Beeston Street, which is a prosperous congregation of Christians. I was granted license as a Marriage Officer by your Excellency on December 11th, No. 6599. I am praying for your permission to continue my work in Jamaica.
> I have the honour to be,
> Your Excellency's obedient Servant,

Industrial College for Colored People, and—in his later years—opened the only black bank in the North. See Wright-Hayre, *Tell Them We Are Rising*.

17. A handwritten note from R. R. Wright Jr. to J. W. Rankin, dated August 3, 1914, states: "I am enclosing you a letter from Jamaica; also two articles and an editorial from the Christian Recorder, which, if you care you may reproduce in the *Voice of Missions*. Hope you will communicate with Bro. Dumar" (*A.M.E. Church Records*, Box 39).

18. Smith, *African Methodist Episcopal Church*, 2:251. During the 1908 General Conference, Bishop C. T. Schaffer introduced the Rev. W. B. Pierson (also spelled Pearson) of Jamaica as a new missionary charged with expanding the presence of the A.M.E. Church on the island of Jamaica during the Home and Foreign Missionary Society session.

THE ALLEN-WESLEYAN LEGACY IN JAMAICA

Another brief self-description of Dumar occurred in the annually printed *Who's Who in Jamaica*, The entry is listed as,

> DUMAR, Alfonso B.D. Minister of Religion. Born at Bath, Maine, U.S.A., on the 3rd August, 1862. Son of Alfonso and Marie Dumar; twice married, present wife was Mrs. Georgia Fox-Livingstone, B.A. Educated at Wilberforce University, Ohio. Minister of the Organization and the Incorporation of the A.M.E. Church in Jamaica. Was an ardent supporter of, and voted for President W. Wilson. Recreations: Good smoke, and long walk. Address: 43 Bond Street, Kingston, P.O.[19]

These descriptions provide an illustration of a cultured man in mid-years, who was somewhat of a risk taker, willing to take the risk of relocating to a foreign country[20]. He was a male Negro born in Bath, Maine, and educated in Ohio—which infers that he probably escaped the worst atrocities of black life in the South, as well as the indignity of menial labor. Dumar would have been a young teenager when the realization that Reconstruction had failed would become apparent to African Americans. Certainly, as an underclassman at Wilberforce, he would have its social implications instilled in his consciousness. As a Wilberforce graduate, he would be encultured in the themes of its motto: "by one's own toil, effort, courage" to elevate the image of the Negro race through an example of moral living, rigorous work ethic, and spiritual fortitude.

Cultivating the Nineteenth-Century Black Elite

At the dawn of the Harlem Renaissance, Dumar was a middle-aged man, and as his missionary work in Jamaica progressed, numerous articles in the *Jamaican Gleaner* invited the public to cultured events sponsored by the A.M.E. Church, which were tailored to attract persons who constituted the elite among twentieth-century Jamaican society. His acceptance among

---

19. Hill, *Who's Who in Jamaica*, 57. This first issue of this serial publication was printed in 1916. Dumar's entry is present from the first issue, in 1916, through 1930. Dumar apparently got into severe trouble with the leadership of the A.M.E. Church in the early 1930s. He was defrocked, and would later align himself with the National Baptist denomination in Jamaica. The circumstances that determined the removal of his ministerial privileges in the A.M.E. Church are not yet clear.

20. I have heard that Dumar had Jamaican parentage but have seen no evidence to support that claim, or suspect that as a reason he would be comfortable with a move in his mature years—other than missionary zeal.

REBAPTISM CALMLY CONSIDERED

the upper crust is exemplified in 1919 Christmas advertisement featured in *The Gleaner*:

> *SOLLAS' SOUVENIR XMAS AND NEW YEAR MAGAZINE.*
> The above named magazine is making
> its appearance for the first time in Jamaica.
> It is intended to advertise to merchants
> of Kingston and country parts and it consists of only
> reliable advertisers as well as articles written by
> Hon. J. P. L. Simpson, JP, OPE,
> His Worship, the Mayor, Mr. R.W. Bryant, JP, MBE,
> Mr. E. A. H. Haggart, Rev S. Solomon,
> Hon. S. Stedman, MLC, for Portland,
> Rev. Alfonso Dumar, Mr. Nath Parker, Mr. Arthur Nicholas,
> Miss P. Davis, Mr. A. Bain Alves, Mr. W. Hinthcliffe, and others.
> It also contains songs and jokes
> and photographs of the King and Queen and others.
> The paper is well printed and nicely got up, and reflects credit on the enterprise of the compiler, Mr. Joshua A. M. Sollas. The well-known Printer of Kingston.
> We commend this pamphlet to the public of Jamaica.[21]

Until recently, the majority of the academy concluded that the African American community did not produce any significant artistic creativity, or display signs of intellectual acuity before the Harlem Renaissance. How then is Dumar's acceptance among the privileged twentieth-century Jamaicans—who were necessarily oriented to British cultural sensitivities explained? Wilson J. Moses argues that it is important to recognize that the Harlem Renaissance was but a continuity of an understated black tradition of literacy and culture. This overlooked tradition lacked the cultural innovation that marked the Harlem Renaissance, to the contrary, it was considered to be quite preservationist[22].

The preservationist center for literacy and culture found its base centered among the black elite of Washington, DC, Writers and scholars were found among the group however,

---

21. Advertisement in *Jamaica Gleaner*, December 24, 1919.
22. Moses, "Lost World of the Negro," 63.

THE ALLEN-WESLEYAN LEGACY IN JAMAICA

> Literate culture in Washington was dominated by flinty old black nationalist preachers who had come of age before or during the Civil War.... They took their politics seriously, preached the necessity of adjusting to industrial democracy, and advocated temperance. Black literary activity in turn of the century Washington was centered around literary societies that the churches sponsored. These literary clubs were of great importance as the framework for some of the important structures of the Harlem Renaissance. Black bourgeois literary institutions prepared the way for Garveyism, the Association for the Study of Negro Life and History, and the NAACP—all of which eventually established journals that published black authors during the Harlem Renaissance.[23]

Counted among those rugged, mature Black Nationalist preachers who had come of age before or during the Civil War, were certainly A.M.E. bishops and leading A.M.E. clergymen, two of the most influential were Bishop Daniel Payne and Henry McNeal Turner. In 1862, Payne assigned Turner to the large and prestigious charge of Israel Church in Washington, DC, the leading A.M.E. Church in the nation's capital. As pastor of Israel Chapel in Washington, DC, Turner quickly made himself known as a powerful preacher and capable pastor among the movers and the shakers in the city. He joined the Prince Hall branch of black freemasons even though there was a strong anti-Masonic movement within the A.M.E. Church (freemasonry was despised by Bishop Daniel Payne). He became well known within political circles, and was befriended by several powerful Republicans, Secretary of the Treasury Salmon Chase, Senators Ben Wade and Charles Sumner, and Representative Thaddeus Stevens. At the time Turner was assigned to Israel Chapel, the Civil War was in full gear, and the Confederate Army had acquired a considerable advantage, having won many of the initial battles in 1861 under the able command of General Robert E. Lee. Therefore, these Republicans and others would often address African-Americans to rally their political support from the pulpit of Israel Chapel A.M.E. Church. Acquiring these political connections would serve Turner well throughout his life and placed him in strategic position of leadership as a prominent political spokesperson on behalf of blacks.

In late 1862, President Lincoln implemented the Emancipation Proclamation, the two-part executive order that made the end of slavery a principle war objective. The proclamation warned slaveholders of the rebel states that he would declare their slaves free unless they laid down their

---

23. Moses, "Lost World of the Negro," 67.

REBAPTISM CALMLY CONSIDERED

arms by January 1, 1863. After this announcement, Turner issued "A Call to Action" to the A.M.E. Church—which reminded its members of the awesome responsibility which was about to befall them.[24] As a pastor he had begun to notice the increase of the number of slaves escaping from their Confederate masters. Many would come to Israel Chapel in need of clothing, food and medical care. These runaway slaves were commonly called 'contraband,' perhaps as a reticent reminder of the designation of runaway slaves who fled slavery to fight for the British during the Revolutionary War.[25] In response, A.M.E. churches combined their efforts and formed the Union Relief Association of Israel Bethel Church, in Washington, DC, in order to effectively provide aid for them. The Union Army began to actively recruit black soldiers. Turner became an enthusiastic recruiter and was rewarded by receiving an appointment as the first black chaplain in the United States Army. This post required him to leave the pastorate of Israel Chapel after having been there just over a year, but he did so willingly, as he had won the support of his congregation by: conducting major physical renovations to the church within his first six months; exposing them to the best academic, religious and political minds in the area; and having consistently preached well.

As presiding bishop, Daniel Payne kept close watch over this influential pulpit and personally endorsed the literary club to maintain its influence among prestigious blacks in the city. Therefore, the A.M.E. Church was at the center, if not the fundamental base for the cultural movement that Moses describes as the Washington Renaissance that "predated the one in Harlem by at least twenty years."[26] Turner was well admired by Dumar, so much, in fact that in a missionary correspondence to Rankin, Dumar states that he intends to model his missionary activity after Turner's work in Georgia.[27] It is not a stretch to imagine that Turner and Dumar may have

24. *Christian Recorder*, October 4, 1862; Walker, *Rock in a Weary Land*, 47–48.
25. McPherson, "Who Freed the Slaves?," 1–10.
26. Moses, "Lost World of the Negro," 65.
27. Bishop Payne appointed Turner as a missionary to the South just after North's Union Army won the Civil War. Turner worked tirelessly to increase the presence of the A.M.E. Church in Georgia, and indeed the Georgia A.M.E. District owes its presence to the strong missionary effort that Turner expended. His approach was much the same, to approach the separate black M.E., South churches and invite them to become a part of the independent A.M.E. denomination. For the most part, after he shared the story of the founding of the A.M.E. Church with the congregation and preached a rousing sermon—the people flocked to join. Turner would later be charged with recklessly licensing preachers without having properly trained them. In a letter to the Secretary of Missions,

had an occasion to meet when Dumar was a young student at Wilberforce or at various A.M.E. conferences across the connectional church. The ethnic consciousness fueled by the black literary movement in Washington, DC, that Moses describes was exemplified in the leadership of the A.M.E. Church at the turn of the century. Hence, when Dumar arrived in Kingston, Jamaica in 1914, with a similarly educated wife who was a classically trained musician, he was ready to command the attention of the members of Kingston's high society, in order to make his appeal for African Methodism on the island of Jamaica.

Pan-African/Pan Nationalist Impulses

Ernest Allen Jr., states that the turn of the century progressive movement was self-contradictory with regard to the plight of African-Americans. "On the one hand, it contributed to the spread of reform sentiments, such as that marked by the formation of the all-black Niagara Movement in 1905. . . . On the other hand the reform spirit balked at any suggestion of African American civic equality."[28] The Pan-Nationalist sentiment found its most recognized distinct expression within the UNIA, Marcus Garvey's Movement which moved its headquarters from Marcus Garvey's native country, Jamaica to Harlem.[29] A very important connection may have occurred between Rev. Alfonso Dumar and Marcus Garvey during a UNIA meeting in 1914.

> THE GLEANER, TUESDAY, SEPTEMBER 22, 1914.
>
> To-night the Universal Negro Improvement Association hold their musical and literary meeting in the Collegiate Hall, commencing at 7 o'clock. The visitor of the evening will be the Rev. Alfonso Dumar who will deliver an address. The programme is made up of interesting items, and among those to contribute the same are Miss C. Mitchell, Mr. Anderson, Mr. White, and Mr. Marcus Garvey. A cordial invitation is extended to the public.[30]

Dumar indicated that he would use Turner's approach in Jamaica. See Angell, *Bishop Henry McNeal Turner*, 60–80.

28. Allen, "New Negro," 52.

29. I found it interesting that Marcus Garvey was baptized into the Wesleyan Methodist Church at St. Ann's Bay, in the parish of St. Ann, Jamaica. See the Garvey Chronology in Hill, *Marcus Garvey and UNIA Papers*, cix.

30. *Jamaica Gleaner*, September 22, 1914.

REBAPTISM CALMLY CONSIDERED

Robert A. Hill lays out the factors that comprised the Garvey movement in, *The Marcus Garvey And Universal Negro Improvement Association Papers*. In the first volume, Hill includes a September 25th, 1914, *Gleaner* article that reported the above-mentioned affair, "The Rev. Alfonso Dumar, was the guest of the evening, and he delivered an eloquent and interesting address which was greatly appreciated by the large and enthusiastic audience." Hill notates the article's inclusion with this insightful footnote,

> Dumar later spoke at a UNIA meeting in New York in June 1924, saying, 'Twelve years ago it was his good fortune to sail to Jamaica from the United States of America and the second public meeting he addressed in the Island Of Jamaica was a meeting at which the Hon. Marcus Garvey was Presiding, a meeting of the Universal Negro Improvement Association. . . . He remembered visiting the office of Mr. Garvey on Charles Street in the City of Kingston and intimating to him that his scheme was a mammoth one that Jamaica was too small to put over, and that if he went to The United States he would find himself inside of ten years at the head of Greatest Negro movement ever inaugurated in the world.[31]

It can be debated to the degree that Dumar's 'counsel' was heard and regarded by Marcus Garvey. Regardless of the ambiguity—it is clear that an encounter between the two men did occur, in which Dumar would have been Garvey's senior—52 years to Garvey's 37 years. Such an encounter was meaningful enough to have been sustained by an additional one in the United States over a decade later, in which Dumar was allowed to speak and his words published in *Negro World*, the official UNIA publication.[32] Liz Mackie offers a description of Garvey's New York based movement, "Garvey's UNIA took up the threads of existing Pan-Africanist ideas, taped the current resentment in the black population and became the major political expression of black discontent."[33]

The expression of black discontent, and any form of black activism which sullied the reality of patriotism among black Americans (particularly in the minds of liberal white Americans) made Alain Locke and many other blacks uncomfortable with the Garvey movement.[34] At a time when

---

31. Hill, *Marcus Garvey and UNIA Papers*, 1:73–74.

32. Dumar may have been prone to hyperbole, having allowed him to be introduced in print, to Kingston at large, as an Attorney-at-law, when he had not matriculated into Law School.

33. Mackie, *Great Marcus Garvey*, 26.

34. Bishop C. S. Smith of the A.M.E. Church was opposed to the Garvey movement.

THE ALLEN-WESLEYAN LEGACY IN JAMAICA

racial tension was at an all time high, many blacks who agreed with Locke's perspective did not want bitterness to increase between blacks and whites. Locke addressed this predicament,

> American nerves in sections unstrung with race hysteria are often fed the opiate that the trend of the Negro advance is wholly separatist, and that the effect of its operation will be to encyst the Negro as a benign foreign body in the body politic. . . . Democracy itself is obstructed and stagnated to the extent that any of its channels are closed. . . . We realize that we cannot be undone without America's undoing. It is within the gamut of this attitude that the thinking Negro faces America, but with variations of mood that are if anything more significant than the aptitude itself. . . . Only the steadying and sobering effect of a truly characteristic gentleness of spirit prevents the rapid rise of a definite cynicism, counter-hate and a defiant superiority feeling. . . . Fortunately, there are constructive channels opening out into which the balked social feelings of the American Negro can flow freely.[35]

What Locke stressed most was the cultural dimension of Black experience—be it politics, aesthetics or even economic life. As a philosopher, Alain Locke's attraction to the Negro artistic aesthetic was centered in authentic interest in form and style, rather than its usefulness for race propaganda. This is the juncture that many of Locke's critics emerge and criticize his definition of race-consciousness, and circumscribed space for Negro art as being elitist and inadequate. Marcus Garvey and W.E. B. DuBois were strong proponents of the use of Negro art as propaganda in the New Negro movement. Locke's *New Negro* was to use art as a vehicle to attain Truth. Therefore, the New Negro must be viewed as a thinking, productive contributor to American culture and democracy at large—free unbridled

---

Robert Hill includes a letter dated, June 25, 1919, from Smith to A. Mitchell Palmer, then the U.S. Attorney General, to whom he sent a copy of *Negro World*. He provides this observation of Marcus Garvey: "I had a lengthy interview with him at my home. As the result of the interview, I am firmly convinced that he is an adventurer and a grafter, bent on exploiting his people to the utmost limit. . . . He is in every respect a 'Red,' according to the sense in which that term is used in the common parlance of the day. He should either be required to discontinue his present vicious propaganda and fake practice or be deported as an undesirable." Smith's view of Garvey may have influenced his interest in Dumar's missionary work in Jamaica. Bishop Smith was assigned to preside over the West Indies in 1916, and while he was presiding prelate, Dumar wrote several letters to Rankin that complain of Smith's lack of support, if not opposition to his Jamaica missionary endeavor. See Hill, *Who's Who in Jamaica*, 446.

35. Locke, *New*, 12–14.

passion and inclinations of revenge. Locke was convinced that the *New Negro's* self-representation through a means of dignified cultural expression that is both authentic to the Negro experience and excellent in form, would force white America to reconsider the subordination of blacks throughout US history. "The especially cultural recognition they win should in turn prove the key to that revaluation of the Negro which much precede or accompany any considerable further betterment of race relationships."[36]

The *New Negro* in the short-lived Harlem Renaissance successfully exposed the literary and artistic giftedness of educated blacks in the 1920s, yet failed to yield the immediate civil rights that Locke had hoped for. It would take several decades and another movement to generate the political will which would affect public policy. An essay penned by W. E. B. DuBois's concludes *The New Negro,* and he summarized the findings of his sociological research as it pertained to his Pan-Africanist ideology. He reiterated that the problem across the globe is the Color Line, and that until racism across the globe is significantly addressed, social unrest and economic oppression will continue to exist.[37] The harsh reality was that for all of its attraction—black intellectuals, writers, and poets failed to establish a viable black middle or upper class. Harlem, like the black migrant, like the New Negro, and like the Renaissance writers did not resolve its own problems, or fulfill its own dreams. Even in Harlem, the Color Line was effectively employed to arrange economic disparity.

Introducing African Methodism

When Dumar arrived in Kingston in 1914, he found a willing audience to hear him share Richard Allen's story of racial uplift, Christian egalitarianism, and self-determination through the principles of African Methodism. The bitter sting of racism had bitten many Jamaicans who had travelled abroad and many had stories of how they had been abused and mistreated as immigrants in England, Panama and the United States. Using the missionary model that Turner set in Georgia, Dumar set about expanding the work by offering connectional affiliation to small independent churches in search of stability. Among the first churches and pastors that eagerly accepted Dumar's offer were small, rural churches, which had been encouraged

---

36. Locke, *New*, 15.
37. DuBois, "Negro Mind Reaches Out," 385–414.

to affiliate with African Methodism through the pioneering efforts of W.B. Pearson.

Dumar printed a self-published pamphlet in 1924, to mark the tenth year of African Methodism on the island of Jamaica. It was titled, *First Bishop of A.M.E. Church: Richard Allen, A Brief Survey of His Life*. The pamphlet concludes with a snippet which records the beginnings of the A.M.E. Church in Jamaica. "African Methodism was organized in the island of Jamaica August 1914 with five preachers and 1,000 members by Rev. Alfonso Dumar, BD, who drew Articles of Incorporation and filed the same. in the office of the Registrar General. The following named ministers and circuits are the starting point: Kingston, Rev. Dumar; Old Harbour, Rev. Bailey; Riversdale, Rev. G.T. Hollar; Temple Hall, Rev. Patterson; Morant Bay, Rev. Williams. Later T.H. Spence united with us."[38] All of these ministers and churches were Independent Native Baptist Churches who were no doubt attracted to the A.M.E. Church because of its history of social protest against racial prejudice and North American connection. It did not take long before the doctrinal issue of baptism had to be publicly addressed by Dumar. Edward W. Lampton, the 31st Bishop of the A.M.E. Church published a concise pamphlet in 1907 titled, *Analysis of Baptism*. The fifty page apologetic document supports the African Methodist Episcopal Church's pedobaptist position. Lampton fundamentally appeals to Scripture to argue his case, for example, in chapter 2, titled, "John's Baptism Not Christian Baptism," Lampton used the scriptural passage from Acts 19: 1–5 to suggest that the apostle Paul's decision to rebaptize persons who had only received baptism from John the Baptist, defeats claims by persons who appeal to John the Baptist as the progenitor of Christian baptism. "Now if the decision of an inspired apostle can settle the question, then it is settled that John's baptism was not Christian baptism."[39] It is very likely that Dumar was familiar with Lampton's work, as it was published the year prior to Lampton's election to the bishopric in 1908. Regardless, Dumar submitted a very telling Letter to the Editor in the November 18th, 1914, issue of the Jamaica Gleaner, in which he states,

> My attention was called to a statement that a baptism was conducted by the Rev. W. T. Bailey, under the auspices of the A.M.E. Church City Mission. And that at said baptism the Rev. gentleman is quoted as having said that he contended that baptism is the only

---

38. Dumar, *First Bishop of the A.M.E. Church*, 14.
39. Lampton, *Analysis of Baptism*, 15.

method by which a person can enter into Christ's Church. I wish to say that:

> The baptism mentioned was not in connection with the City Mission of the African Methodist Episcopal 52 Beeston Street
>
> That the African Methodist Episcopal do not teach that baptism by emersion is the only means by which a person can enter into Christ's Church.... As the Superintendent of Missions of the African Methodist Episcopal Church in Jamaica, we don't want the reading public to be mis-informed to the doctrine of this denomination. As it is now generally understood that the City Mission A.M.E. is that at 52 Beeston Street, at which place the pure and unadulterated doctrine of the A.M.E. Church is taught and infant baptism is one of the leading tenents [sic] of the church.

I am, etc

Alfonso Dumar

52 Beeston Street,

Kingston

Nov. 17th 1914.[40]

Dumar's prompt editorial response publicly communicated the A.M.E. Church's denominational commitment to pedobaptism. However, it was not sufficient to overturn the private commitment of many leaders and members within the A.M.E. Churches of Jamaica to Jamaican religiosity and its ideological adherence to believer's baptism.

Contextual Influence of Bedwardism

Rev. W. Theo Bailey was in fact, one of the founding members of the A.M.E. Church as mentioned in Dumar's recollection of the beginning of the work in Jamaica. As an established pastor of a moderate sized congregation in Old Harbour, he was merely reciting a well-accepted fact within popular African Jamaican religiosity when the seemingly 'problematic' baptism occurred. The observations of Marsha Warren Beckwith, Vassar professor, and acclaimed ethnographer and specialist in folklore, provide a helpful snapshot of the popular religious landscape from a North American viewpoint. Beckwith's essay, "Some Revival Cults in Jamaica," highlight three important religious groups of importance in her estimation, the Revivalists, the Isaiahs, and the Bedwardites. Beckwith gives the most attention to the

---

40. *Jamaica Gleaner*, 18 November 1914.

THE ALLEN-WESLEYAN LEGACY IN JAMAICA

Bedwardites, followed by the Revivalists, and finally only two and a half paragraphs pertain to the Isaiahs. The Bedwardites are the most dynamic and charismatic group of the three.[41] Social historians of Jamaica consider Alexander Bedward to be the last major influential Native Baptist leader in the twentieth century. His ministry paid homage to a tradition of Jamaican Native Baptist resistance against injustice and oppression from the era of slavery through the nation's stirrings for political independence from England. Beckwith observed that both the Revivalists and the Bedwardites used water as a major ritual element, but failed to provide much useful information. George Simpson offers a bit more insight, "While the principal water ritual was baptism . . . glasses, jars and pools of consecrated are evident in . . . revivalist churches . . . [for other spiritual benefits]. Additional uses of water include: attracting certain spirits to a service, driving away evil spirits, healing, divining, and duppy catching."[42] Camille Tounouga cites that while water is a subject of scientific research and the object of conflicts, it is above all, an element that profoundly affects humanity's imagination. She argues that three models for the representation of water are found in Sub-Saharan African traditions: water as a source of life, as an instrument of purification and as a source for regeneration. Throughout Black Africa, water is understood as the realm of the spirits and the birthplace of creation, therefore its symbolization is thoroughly embedded in religion, spirituality, legends and rituals.[43]

Bedward's ministry had an unusual approach to the use of water. According to A.A. Brooks, his biographer, Bedward was chosen to assume leadership of the Native Baptist Free Church, (a church established by a mysterious American minister named Shakespeare) in August Town, St. Andrew, Jamaica. Shakespeare designated Bedward to be his successor in 1901, just before he died. August Town is an impoverished district surrounded by mountains with the Mona River nearby. Born in 1859, Bedward had been plagued with a chronic illness for years. He received relief when he travelled to work in Panama, but while there he received a vision along with a divine mandate to return to Jamaica—to get baptized or risk death. He did return and was baptized in 1885. His ministry officially began in October 1891, and "On the 22nd Dec., 1891, A. Bedward made his first public performance at the Mona River, dispensing the water as medicine,

---

41. Beckwith, *Black Roadways*, 9–11.
42. Simpson, "Acculturative Process," 336.
43. Tounouga, "Symbolic Function of Water," 283–84.

and baptizing."⁴⁴ Thus, Bedward introduced an innovative use of water in popular African Jamaican religiosity, using water as medicine for physical ailments. Brooks defended the practice,

> In the month of June 1893, the water of the Mona River, Augusttown which Bedward upon Divine Revelation, claimed to be and dispensed as medicine, was tested by the Government. . . . Is it not on public declaration and government record, that it contains every medicinal quality, excepting castor oil? Poor uneducated Bedward never knew what the water contained. He only knew that the Lord told him saying: 'Once I made water wine, behold! Now I make water medicine. And you have I ordained my Dispenser, Watchman, Shepherd and Trumpeter.'
>
> Though deficient in scientific knowledge Bedward was adequate in faith. . . . There are those who say they do not believe the water is medicinal, for they have seen no cure effected by it. . . . But the fame and the popularity of the medicinal water must have some ground or cause. . . . Since 1889 it has been holding its own. . . . Volumes could not contain the names of many who suffered affliction for years, consulted many doctors, and spent many pounds all in vain. Finally, they tried Augusttown medicinal water by bathing or drinking or both and have been made whole.⁴⁵

Brooks goes on to explain Bedwardism as being characterized as a community of believers who hold to a strict observance of Fasting and Prayer as well as the Vow Ceremony. "The first formal step into church membership in the case of persons to be baptized is the 'Vow.'"⁴⁶ The fasting ceremony occurred on Monday, Wednesday and Friday, and members were expected to gather dressed in white with white tea cups and saucers, at long rows of tables draped in white tablecloths. The mood was somber and reflected austere British colonial, if not Victorian emotive restraint. Ele-

---

44. Brooks, *History of Bedwardism*, 7. Brooks's date may be off with regard to the beginning of Bedward's ministry. Most scholars cite 1895 as the year when Bedward's ministry began. The titles Shepherd, Watchman, and Trumpeter were used frequently in early twentieth-century Revivalism. The title Dispenser may be unique to Bedward. Lastly, a commitment to defeat white oppression would mark Bedward's ministry. He was arrested in 1921 for preaching sedition, "that blacks should rise up and overthrow White domination" (Stewart, *Three Eyes for the Journey*, 114). His only exposure to significant oppression from whites would have occurred when he worked as a laborer in Panama. It was only after Marcus Garvey worked in Colon, Panama, that he began to develop his Pan-Africanist vision of the UNIA.

45. Brooks, *History of Bedwardism*, 9.

46. Brooks, *History of Bedwardism*, 14.

THE ALLEN-WESLEYAN LEGACY IN JAMAICA

ments of bread and medicinal water from the Mona River were placed at the head of the table, where the presiding minister would sit. After a singing of a hymn, reading a Scripture and prayer, the elements were blessed and the elements would be served as the congregation sat. Bedward explained the fasting ceremony to Beckwith as one in which the heart was regularly cleansed—just as a person regularly washed their clothes.[47]

The most significant teaching of the Native Baptist Free Church that Brooks presents is the teleological view. "As Judaism was succeeded by Christianity, so Christianity is being succeeded by Bedwardism."[48] This teleological line of reasoning was worked through to its eschatological conclusion with a dramatic prophecy from Bedward. In 1920, Bedward assumed a new title—that of "Lord," as opposed to Shepherd—and began to identify himself as an incarnation of the crucified Jesus Christ. Bedward's experience in Colon had provided him with an intolerance for injustice, while other ministers were allowed to become lawful Marriage Officers, and perform marriages, Bedward and his ministers were repeatedly denied the privilege. For poor Jamaican laborers who lacked wealth, Christian marriage was a highly estimated mark of morality and respectability, and the denial of Bedward the right to marry his members relegated them to social marginalization. "Marriage celebrant status had 'been definitely denied him, and he had accordingly decided to bring the world to an end.'"[49]

An imminent millennialism began to infiltrate his teaching and preaching. Millennialism is the expectation of the harmonious state that will occur when the kingdom of God is realized on earth when Christ's reign of one thousand years transpires. Throughout Christendom the expectation of this occurrence has varied from urgent expectation of Christ's immediate return, or patient, but diligent watchfulness for his delayed coming. Notwithstanding, the scripture references most cited as related to Christ's return are the series of violent events as cited in the synoptic Gospels (Matt 24; Mark 13; Luke 21); and the miraculous event of Christ's

---

47. See Beckwith, *Black Roadways*, 44, 45; Austin-Broos, *Jamaica Genesis*, 83–85. Austin-Broos compares the Native Baptist Free Church's tri-weekly fasting ceremony to an Anglican Communion service. I am inclined to believe, however, that the elements of bread and water—with its intention to 'clean the heart'—more closely resemble the Wesleyan Methodist Love Feast. Brooks provides documents that Bedward's church did fellowship occasionally with August Town Wesleyan Methodist and Baptist Churches, while stating that the Anglican Church failed to respond to their invitations.

48. Brooks, *History of Bedwardism*, 17.

49. Austin-Broos, *Jamaica Genesis*, 86.

return and gathering of the Church, the *parousia* as described by Paul (1 Thess 4:16–18). Beckwith provides an eyewitness account,

> Upon reaching Kingston in December 1920, I found the city in a state of half-amused, half-expectant excitement because a certain Negro prophet named Alexander Bedward had predicted his own ascent into heaven, the destruction of the whites, and the reign of Bedwardism upon earth. These climactic events were to take place on the last day of December of that very year. The faithful were exhorted to gather into the village of August Town, at the foot of the Port Royal mountains near the river Mona, a few miles out of Kingston, where stood Bedward's church and where for thirty-two years had centered those religious activities of the prophet which had made the "healing stream" of the Mona river and the baptisms held in its life-giving waters celebrated all over the island and had gathered a large number of converts to his teaching. In response to the prophet's call, those living in other parts of the island were now rapidly selling out whatever of their property was not transferable and flocking to the central camp at August Town to be ready for the predicted destruction, which was to fall upon none, white or black, who stood within the sacred enclosure destined to become the center of the new Jerusalem. . . . Even the intelligent whites believed that something out of the ordinary was about to happen. Among educated colored people I heard one reminding another wistfully of another Christmas day and of another prophet who was to the wise foolishness but whom the common folk had heard gladly. The negro entertainer at the Flamstead estate where I spent Christmas day, enumerating the marked events in his life said, "I remember the St. Thomas rebellion in [1865] and the Revival of 1860. It was taken up by the whole world. Now to-day there is Bedward!"[50]

Bedward's millennial prophecies would fail to materialize on the specified date, and he would reschedule the apocalyptic event repeatedly, until he was declared insane and assigned to the Bellevue Mental Asylum where he would live out his last days, and die in 1930. Nevertheless, Bedward's memory is revered by many as the Native Baptist anti-colonial champion of resistance against colonial domination. Barry Chevannes argues that the Rastafarians would develop their colonial critique from Bedward, but instead of using ritual to cure the affliction of social injustice and

---

50. Beckwith, *Black Roadways*, 3.

THE ALLEN-WESLEYAN LEGACY IN JAMAICA

immorality, would turn to knowledge of Africa to confront the ills of European colonialism.[51]

Bedward is viewed by many as a martyr in the Jamaican Revival tradition, and is often remembered as one who was persecuted for his anticolonial views and his charismatic hold over many followers. Austin-Broos records, "At least for a first few decades of the [twentieth] century, 'Bedwardite' became a census category of the Jamaican government and numbered in 1921 almost as many affiliates as the category "Church of God."[52] Alfonso Dumar's earliest congregations and minister's may not have been Bedwardite, and there is no indication that the two men actually met, however, it is clear that Christian myalism of the Native Baptist tradition was the tradition in which most of the first A.M.E. ministers were trained. In a move similar to George Liele, Dumar quickly sought to minimize the unorthodox Africanisms and sway the doctrinal balance by seeking to add trained ministers and congregations from United Methodist Free Churches who were no longer being supported by their British parent organization. Dumar's wooing efforts are seen as early as January 1915, at the auspicious occasion when the first A.M.E. bishop visits Jamaica to review the missionary work.

THE GLEANER, SATURDAY, JANUARY 16, 1915.
Rt. Rev. Dr. John Hurst
And Dr. J. W. Rankin
At Old Harbour.

Old Harbour, Jan. 14—His Lordship Bishop John Hurst, DD, and the Rev. Dr. J. W. Rankin in company with the Rev. Alfonso Dumar, BD, arrived at Old Harbour on Wednesday the 13th. They were met at the railway station by the Rev. Mr. Bailey, who conducted them to the Bay on a visit to the circuit. The gentlemen were charmed with this part of the island and expressed the joy It gave them to visit the picturesque scenery of this beautiful island. Their only sorrow was the fact of their short stay.

At 7 p.m., a great crowd assembled at the Zion Church to hear them. On the platform, associated with the divines were the pastor of the church presiding. Rev. G.L. Young of Brown's Hall and A. Dumar of Allen's Temple. After a hymn was sung and prayer

---

51. See Chevannes, *Rastafarianism*.
52. Austin-Broos, *Jamaica Genesis*, 86.

offered by Mr. Dumar, the choir rendered a welcome air and the pastor read an address of welcome from the Church.[53]

The Rev. G. L. Young of Brown's Hall was a well-respected member of Kingston society, and leading pastor of the United Methodist Free Church. His presence on the rostrum along with Bishop Hurst and Secretary of Mission, Dr. Rankin, is evidence that Dumar was cultivating his friendship and trust to gain his membership and thus subsequent social respectability for the A.M.E. Church. Rev. Young would affiliate with the A.M.E. Church, however, not before making several complaints about the overwhelming presence of Native Baptist influence in the A.M.E. Church. For example, this illustrious meeting was held at Rev. W. T. Bailey's church at Old Harbour, and the name of his church was Zion A.M.E. Church, a literal reminder of its ties with Revival Zion heritage.

Organization of the Jamaica Mission Conference

According to a public address given by W. T. Bailey, during Bishop Hurst's visit, Dumar appears to have strengthened and built upon the work of W. B. Pearson, the previous missionary to Jamaica.

> Mr. Dumar came to the island during 1914 and finding that there was some fabric resembling in name, his fostering mother, tackled the situation. . . . He undertook to visit the different centres where this great Church was operating, preached Christ and spoke to the people in a hopeful and encouraging way and we are certainly pleased to assert that the consummation which this work has attained to up to the instance is due to him.[54]

Jamaica was formerly recognized as a Mission conference within the connectional A.M.E. Church with the visit of Bishop Hurst in 1915.

L. L. Berry, subsequent Secretary of Missions and author of *A Century of Missions of the A.M.E. Church*, recorded, "Since the beginning of the activities of the A.M.E. Church in Jamaica, in 1915, the work has grown to eleven churches with more than 800 members."[55]

---

53. *Jamaica Gleaner*, January 15, 1915. Brown would pass away in 1924, and several years after his death, his former congregation at Brown's Hall withdrew their A.M.E. affiliation and joined the Presbyterian Church.

54. *Jamaica Gleaner*, January 14, 1915.

55. Berry, *Century of Missions*, 199.

THE ALLEN-WESLEYAN LEGACY IN JAMAICA

Dumar's missionary endeavor found fertile ground within Native Baptist congregations seeking financial support and social legitimacy from an established North American denomination. Between Rev. Dumar's first arrival to the island in 1912 and the late 1930s, almost one hundred A.M.E. churches had been established, and with few exceptions, most of these churches were congregations that worshipped in the Native Baptist tradition.[56]

The primary exception was Dumar's personal cathedral and testament to the dignity of African Methodism, Allen Temple in West Kingston. Prior to and during the building of Allen Temple, there is fevered missionary correspondence by Dumar to Rankin, indicating the importance of the work. Dumar's dream is to construct a stately edifice in the island's capital to reflect the dignity of African Methodism. A letter from Dumar to Rankin, dated April 1st, 1916, reveals his excitement:

> I am sending you by this mail an unmounted photo of the Corner Stone laying in this city. The first Corner Stone ever layed for an African Methodist Episcopal Church in Jamaica. Historic by reason of the proposed building is named for the first bishop of the church—Allen Temple and in this centennial year! The crowd was fearful large. Mark the banners and flags on picture! Sir it was a great day for our people. And in this poor island among the poorest people I raised £8 or $40, at this stone laying.[57]

The church would be constructed by Spring 1917, just in time for the new presiding prelate, Bishop C. S. Smith to arrive and admit the Jamaica mission into the West Indies Conference.

> THE NEW TEMPLE.
>
> There was a large turn-out on Sunday last, on the occasion of the opening, of the new Allen Temple A.M.E. Church, of which the Rev. Alfonso Dumar is Pastor. Three services were held, and at each of them, the sacred edifice was filled to overflowing. At the 11 o'clock service, the Rev. T. Gordon Somers delivered a most eloquent sermon; at 3 p.m. the congregation had the pleasure of listening to the Rev. Theo Bailey, whilst the Rev. G. L. Young was the special preacher at night. The new building certainly reflects the

---

56. Numerous congregations affiliated with the A.M.E. church and then quickly departed once they realized that they would be required to abandon much of their Revivalist practices and/or sign over their property to the North American connectional church.

57. *A.M.E. Church Records*, Box 39, s.v. Dumar Folder.

great credit on Mr. Dumar and his co-workers. It is a fine structure and is well equipped for the service of the Master.[58]

Two additional articles in this issue of the *Jamaica Gleaner* were printed to indicate the recent and impending activities of the A.M.E. Church. The importance of Bishop Smith's presence was highlighted to indicate that the A.M.E. headquarters of the West Indies Conference would be Jamaica, (and by extension, under Dumar's influence). However, the Jamaica Annual Conference would not be officially organized and admitted into the connection as an independent entity until 1921. Bishop R. R. Wright Jr., documents the following,

> The A.M.E. Church was brought to Jamaica in 1912 by Alphanso Dumar. . . . Of the work done in nine years which followed, no account can be given, but on November 1921, our conference was reorganized at Allen Temple. Present were Bishop William A. Fountain, newly elected bishop.[59]

Infant Baptism in Hot Water

The organization of the Jamaican Annual Conference unintentionally legitimized the merger between the North American A.M.E. Church and the Jamaican Native Baptist tradition. There was little indication of doctrinal conflict, however, the rite of baptism highlights the distinctions of culture, doctrine and liturgical practice between the two. Dumar's correspondence in the Jamaica Gleaner provides insight into how he gingerly navigated the tension between the two perspectives. Shortly after the November 1914 article in which Dumar publicly condemns Bailey's actions and words, we find him advertising his baptisms by immersion.

> THE GLEANER, SATURDAY, APRIL 10, 1915.
>
> Last Sunday night, the Rev. Alfonso Dumar, BD, preached to a crowded house at Allen Temple A.M.E. Church, at which service sixty-one persons took Holy Communion. He will baptize sixteen persons by immersion on the third Sunday in May.

It is important to note that Dumar was not holding his services in a church, therefore he had no sanctuary in which to perform baptisms.

---

58. *Jamaica Gleaner*, March 1, 1917.
59. Wright Jr., *Sixteenth Episcopal District*, 85.

THE ALLEN-WESLEYAN LEGACY IN JAMAICA

After Allen Temple was constructed in 1917, we note that Dumar begins to advertise infant baptisms in the section of the Jamaica Gleaner reserved for Church Announcements. It appears to be an anomaly, as no other ministers are advertising that practice. For example,

> SATURDAY, NOVEMBER, 2, 1918.
> AFRICAN METHODIST EPISCOPAL CHURCH.
> Allen Temple, 89 Beeston Street—
> 11 Rev. Alfonso Dumar, BD, *Infant Baptism*;
> 3 Junior League; 6 Christian Endeavour League;
> 7 Rev. Alfonso Dumar, BD.[60]

Rather quickly, it becomes apparent that Dumar did not make allowances for the necessity of a pool in his new sanctuary, as we find a subsequent advertisement,

> THE GLEANER, SATURDAY, JULY 31, 1920
>
> Sunday morning, 6:30 a.m., the Rev. Alfonso Dumar will baptise by immersion in Hope River a class of seven candidates. Public invitation to all.[61]

This advertisement betrays the acculturation that Dumar assented to as an A.M.E. minister in Jamaica. The baptism advertised did not occur during the scheduled worship service but at daybreak at a riverside, which mimicked the Native Baptist ritual. Dumar would continue to advertise infant baptism in the Gleaner, and confer baptism by immersion upon the adult candidates who required it. Unfortunately, it will never be known how he would have successfully resolved the tension. His defrocking and resignation from the A.M.E. Church is one of the greatest tragedies to have befallen the work on the island.

The preference for the baptismal mode of immersion linked with subjective witness to Christian conversion has been shown to be linked to the Native Baptist Jamaican tradition which was the unexpected consequence of George Liele's missionary effort to Jamaica in the late eighteenth and early nineteenth centuries. Evidence has been presented which demonstrates the influence of traditional religion of Central and Western Africa upon the Native Baptist tradition in the religio-cultural history of Jamaica. The

---

60. *Jamaica Gleaner*, November 2, 1918.
61. *Jamaica Gleaner*, July 20, 1920.

impact of the Great Revival during the years of 1860 and 1861 on current popular religiosity of many Jamaicans has been described. Furthermore, I have shown how African Methodism in Jamaica exhibits attributes from its Wesleyan and Jamaican Revivalism parents within its praxis of Christian initiation. I have provided a historical survey of the rite of baptism in the Western Church, alongside an example of liturgical innovation within a particular region of fifth-century Christendom. The influence of the Protestant Reformation emerge in Ted Campbell's claims that support the probable influence of mainline Reformed tradition on John Wesley's baptismal thought. Historically, the Wesleyan-Methodist doctrinal commitment to infant baptism alongside the requirement for evangelical conversion has caused no small debate among the branches of the communities of faith which claim to be inheritors of the root of the eighteenth-century Wesleyan revival. The Jamaican context of popular religiosity, and the corresponding of the early A.M.E. church's two-fold liturgical praxis of Christian initiation could be viewed as an additional socio-cultural example, which 'muddies' the orthodox baptismal water of Methodism. This work positions itself along the trajectory of Wesleyan pragmatism and has attempted to present evidence that demonstrates that the Christian initiation rituals within the early A.M.E. Church of Jamaica could be interpreted as being aligned with Wesley's own two-fold view of baptismal regeneration and the requirement of the new birth.

The importance of inculturation and the problems that arise between doctrine and praxis, quickly engaged me during the work of ethnographic research. Ritual studies must take into account, as much as possible, the historical, social, political and economic contexts that affect the people who perform them. As Jeffrey Campbell argued in Cultural Pragmatics, the more complex the society in which the ritual takes place, the greater the necessity for a dynamic and effervescent ritual to create meaning for the performers and observers. Much of Christendom continues to wrestle with the understanding of baptism as a birth rite when the traditional model is that of a rite of initiation into a new way of living. All rituals are continuously in a state of flux, and are no longer characterized as rigidly fixed entities, however, while a ritual innovation may reflect fluidity, its underlying cultural worldview changes at a much slower pace. Within the Church, ritual experimentation effectively operates to the degree that is oriented to one's discovery of personhood and identity through the Wholly Other.

THE ALLEN-WESLEYAN LEGACY IN JAMAICA

Most clergy and members of early Jamaican A.M.E. Churches were comfortable with *two* sacramental rituals that utilized water. The first rite was performed by the mode of sprinkling and the proper subjects were infants. I argue that this ritual is the liturgical contribution of the Rev. Alfonso Dumar, the founder of the A.M.E. Church in Jamaica. It is a liturgical innovation, in the sense that the Revival or Native Baptist tradition had no similar ritual, other than Liele's 'dry-christening' which was very probably a formal Baptist infant dedication service. The insistence upon the use of water and sprinkling babies was emphasized by Dumar and the new rite was adopted by ministers and pastors who had aligned with the A.M.E. Church.

Rebaptism by immersion in the early Jamaican A.M.E. Church was not understood as a violation of orthodoxy because in the Wittgensteinian sense, it didn't follow the rules of the game of semantics. The words, signs and symbols interpreted by the community indicated that immersion wasn't rebaptism, it was simply baptism, the ritual of Christian initiation that imparted full personhood to baptizands, who by their consent became children of God. Descendants of Africa in the wake of the unspeakable horrors of New World Slavery and colonialism would utilize this rite to bathe their black bodies, restore their souls and receive power as new persons created by the Spirit of God to resist the dehumanizing forces of sin and oppression.

BIBLIOGRAPHY

Primary Sources

Acts of the Assembly passed in the Island of Jamaica from 1681 to 1737 inclusive. London: Lewis and Ebberall, 1745.

Acts of the Assembly passed in the Island of Jamaica from 1770 to 1783 inclusive. London: Lewis and Ebberall, 1786.

Allen, Ernest, Jr. "The New Negro: Explorations in Identity and Social Consciousness, 1921-1922." In *The Cultural Moment*, edited by Adele Heller and Lois Rudnick, 48-68. New Brunswick, NJ: Rutgers University Press, 1991.

Allen, Richard. *The Life, Experience, and Gospel Labours of the Rt. Rev. Richard Allen.* Philadelphia: Martin & Boden, 1833.

A.M.E. *Church Records, Home and Foreign Missions.* Boxes 39-44. Schomburg Center for Research in Black Culture. Manuscripts, Archives, & Rare Books Division. New York Public Library. Uncatalogued collection.

Bridges, George W. *Annals of Slavery.* Vol. 1. Kingston: John Murray, 1827.

———. "Rev. G. W. Bridges and his Slave Kitty Hylton." *The Anti-Slavery Monthly Reporter* 3.66 (1830) 373.

———. "Rev. G. W. Bridges on the Effects of Manumission." *Christian Observer* 23.12 (1823) 760-67.

"Court of King's Bench." *The Examiner* (1829). http://www.nationalarchives.gov.uk/court-kings-bench-crown-side-1675-1875.

Hill, William. *Alphabetical Arrangement of all the Wesleyan Methodist Preachers and Missionaries Travelling in Great Britain and Overseas.* 2nd ed. London: John Mason, 1824.

———. *Alphabetical Arrangement of all the Wesleyan Methodist Preachers and Missionaries Travelling in Great Britain and Overseas.* 3rd ed. London: John Mason, 1827.

———. *A Supplement to Hill's Alphabetical Arrangement of the Wesleyan Methodist Preachers and Missionaries belonging to the British Conferences (1826-1832).* London: John Mason, 1833.

Hollar, G. J. "Missionary Correspondence: June 6, 1916." In *A.M.E. Church Records: Home and Foreign Missions Missionary Correspondence*, Box 39. Schomburg Center for Research in Black Culture. New York: unpublished.

BIBLIOGRAPHY

Kerr, David. "An Answer to the Objections of the Reverend Thomas Pennock against 'Methodism as it is.'" *Jamaica Watchman*, June 7, 1837. Reprint, July 5, 1837.

Liele, George, et al. "Letters Showing the Rise and Progress From the Early Negro Preachers of Georgia and the West Indies." *The Journal of Negro History* 1.1 (1916) 69–92.

"Minutes of the Home and Foreign Missionary Society." *Voice of Missions* 1.1 (1893) 1.

Pennock, Thomas. "Charges alleged against the Sectarians by certain Senators in the Jamaica House of Assembly, 30th November 1830." s.n., 1830.

———. "Reasons for using our Utmost Exertions to Procure the Abolition of Slavery: An Extract From the Speech of the Rev. Mr. Pennock, a West Indian Missionary." *Newcastle Courant*, May 2, 1829.

———. "The Rev. Pennock's Withdrawal From Methodism As It Is: Letter I." *Royal Gazette*, May 31, 1837.

———. "The Rev. Pennock's Withdrawal From Methodism As It Is: Letter II." *Royal Gazette*, June 10, 1837.

———. *Sermon to the Apprentices on the First Anniversary of their Freedom from Slavery: Preached in the Wesleyan Chapel, Montego Bay, Jamaica, on Sunday, August 2, 1835*. Kingston, JA: Jordan and Osborne, 1836.

Tanner, Benjamin T. *Apology for African Methodism*. Baltimore: DGH&M, 1867.

Wesley, John. *Bicentennial Edition of the Works of John Wesley*. Edited by Frank Baker and Richard P. Heitzenrater. Nashville: Abingdon, 1976.

———. *Doctrine of Original Sin, According to Scripture, Reason, and Experience*. Bristol: Farley, 1757.

———. *Preservative Against Unsettled Notions in Religion*. Bristol: E. Farley, 1758.

Wesleyan Methodist Missionary Society (WMMS). *Missionary Correspondence: West Indies and Jamaica, 1803–1840*. Text-fiche.

MAGAZINES AND NEWSPAPERS

The Christian Recorder, the periodical of the A.M.E. Church, 1874–1920.

The Jamaica Gleaner, Jamaica's oldest continuously published newspaper, 1912–1936.

The Jamaica Watchman, Jamaica Free Press, and other local newspapers, 1829–1838.

The Voice of Missions, the missionary journal of the A.M.E. Church which featured letters, progress, and supplications of A.M.E. missionaries around the world, 1893–1900.

Secondary Sources

African Methodist Episcopal Church. *2016 Doctrine and Discipline of the African Methodist Episcopal Church: Bicentennial Edition*. Nashville: AMEC, 2016.

African Methodist Episcopal Church. *Bicentennial Hymnal*. Nashville: AMEC, 1986.

African Methodist Episcopal Church. *The Doctrine and Discipline of the African Methodist Episcopal Church 2004*. Nashville: AMEC, 2005.

Alexander, Jeffrey C. "Cultural Pragmatics: Social Performance Between Ritual and Strategy." *Sociological Theory* 22.4 (2004) 527–73.

Allen, Ernest. "New Negro: Explorations in Identity and Social Consciousness, 1921–1922." In *The Cultural Moment*, edited by Adele Heller and Lois Rudnick, 48–68. New Brunswick, NJ: Rutgers University Press, 1991.

BIBLIOGRAPHY

Alleyne, Mervyn C. *Africa: Roots of Jamaican Culture*. London: Pluto, 1989.

Anderson, Lesley G. *Baptism, Superstitions, and the Supernatural: A Caribbean Perspective*. Kingston, JA: Faith Works, 2010.

Angell, Stephen Ward. *Bishop Henry McNeal Turner and African American Religion in the South*. Knoxville: University of Tennessee Press, 1992.

Austin-Broos, Diane J. *Jamaica Genesis: Religion and the Politics of Moral Orders*. Chicago: University of Chicago Press, 1997.

Bastide, Roger. *African Civilizations in the New World*. New York: Harper and Row, 1971.

Bay, Edna, and Kristin Mann. *Rethinking the African Diaspora: The Making of a Black Atlantic World in the Bight of Benin and Brazil*. Abingdon, Oxon: Frank Pass, 2001.

Beckerlegge, Oliver. *United Methodist Free Churches: A Study in Freedom*. London: Epworth, 1957.

Beckwith, Martha Warren. *Black Roadways*. New York: Negro Universities Press, 1929.

Benn, Dennis. *Caribbean: An Intellectual History, 1774-2003*. Kingston, JA: Ian Randle, 2004.

Berry, Llewyn L. *Century of Missions of the African Methodist Episcopal Church, 1840-1940*. New York: Gutenberg, 1942.

Bhabha, Homi K. *Location of Culture*. London: Routledge, 1994.

Bilby, Kenneth M. *True Born Maroons*. Gainesville, FL: University Press of Florida, 2005.

Bisnauth, Dale. *History of Religions in the Caribbean*. Kingston, JA: LMH, 1989.

Bleby, Henry. *Death Struggles of Slavery: Being a Narrative of Facts and Incidents which occurred in a British Colony, during the two years Immediately Prior to Negro Emancipation*. London: Hamilton, Davis, and Co., 1853.

Borgen, Ole E. *John Wesley on the Sacraments: A Theological Study*. Nashville: Abingdon, 1972.

Bridge, Donald, and David Phypers. *Water that Divides: The Baptism Debate*. Leicester: InterVarsity, 1977.

Brooks, A. A. *History of Bedwardism*. Kingston, JA: Gleaner, 1917.

Bryant, Kenzie. "The Archbishop Who Baptized Meghan Markle Speaks." *Vanity Fair*. March 16, 2016. https://www.vanityfair.com/style/2018/03/meghan-markle-baptism-wedding-officiant-archbishop-speaks.

Buchner, J. H. *The Moravians In Jamaica: History of the Mission of the United Brethren's Church to the Negroes in Jamaica, 1754-1854*. London: Longman, Brown, and Co., 1854.

Campbell, James T. *Songs of Zion: The African Methodist Episcopal Church in the United States and in South Africa*. New York: Oxford University Press, 1995.

Campbell, Ted A. *Religion of the Heart: A Study of European Religious Life in the Seventeenth and Eighteenth Centuries*. Columbia: University of South Carolina Press, 1991.

———. *Wesleyan Beliefs: Formal and Popular Expressions of the Core Beliefs of Wesleyan Communities*. Nashville: Kingswood, 2010.

Chevannes, Barry. *Rastafarianism, Roots and Ideology*. Syracuse, NY: Syracuse University Press, 1994.

Collins, Kenneth J. *John Wesley: A Theological Journey*. Nashville: Abingdon, 2003.

Cordell, Dennis D., and Joel W. Gregory, eds. *African Population and Capitalism: Historical Perspectives*. Reprint. Madison, WI: University of Wisconsin Press, 1994.

Cone, James. *For My People: Black Theology and the Black Church*. Maryknoll, NY: Orbis, 1984.

BIBLIOGRAPHY

Cooper, Terry D. *Sin, Pride & Self-Acceptance: The Problem of Identity in Theology & Psychology.* Downers Grove, IL: InterVarsity 2003.

Cox, Francis. *History of the Baptist Missionary Society from 1792-1842.* Vol. 2. London: Ward, 1842.

Curnock, Nicholas, ed. *Journal of the Rev. John Wesley, AM.* Vol. 3. London: Epworth, 1938. Originally published in 1912.

Curtin, Phillip. *Two Jamaicas: The Role of Ideas in a Tropical Colony.* Westport, CT: Greenwood, 1968. Originally published in 1955.

Davies, Rupert. *Methodism.* Harmondsworth: Penguin, 1963.

Dick, Devon. *Cross and the Machete. Native Baptists of Jamaica, Identity, Ministry, and Legacy.* Kingston: Ian Randle, 2009.

Dickerson, Dennis. *Reflections on A.M.E. Church History.* Nashville: AME Sunday School Union, 2009.

Dimond, Sydney. *Psychology of the Methodist Revival.* London: Oxford University Press, 1926.

DuBois, W. E. B. "The Negro Mind Reaches Out." In *The New Negro,* edited by Alain Locke, 385-414. New York: Albert and Charles Boni, 1925.

Dumar, Alfonso. *First Bishop of the A.M.E. Church: Richard Allen, A Brief Survey of His Life.* Kingston, JA: self-published, 1924.

Duncan, Peter. *A Narrative of the Wesleyan Mission to Jamaica: With Occasional Remarks on the State of Society on that Island.* London: Partridge and Oakey, 1849.

Edwards, Bryan. *The History, Civil and Commercial, of the British Colonies in the West Indies.* Vol. 2. London: J. Stockdale, 1793.

Erskine, Noel Leo. *Decolonizing Theology: A Caribbean Perspective.* Maryknoll, NY: Orbis, 1981.

———. *Plantation Church: How African American Religion was born in Caribbean Slavery.* London: Oxford University Press, 2014.

Felton, Gayle. *This Gift of Water: The Practice and Theology of Baptism among Methodists in America.* Nashville: Abingdon, 1992.

Ferguson, Everett. *Baptism in the Early Church: History, Theology and Liturgy in the first Five Centuries.* Cambridge: Eerdmans, 2009.

Findlay, George. *History of the Wesleyan Methodist Missionary Society.* Vol. 2. London: Epworth, 1921.

Finn, Thomas M. *From Death to Rebirth: Ritual and Conversion in Antiquity.* Mahwah, NJ: Paulist, 1997.

Foster, Henry Blaine. *Rise and Progress of Wesleyan Methodism in Jamaica.* London: Wesleyan Conference Office, 1881.

Frazier, Edward Franklin. *The Negro Church in America.* New York: Schocken, 1964.

Frey, Sylvia, and Betty Wood. *Come Shouting to Zion: African-American Protestantism in the American South and the British Caribbean to 1830.* Chapel Hill: University of North Carolina Press, 1998.

Fulop, Timothy E., and Albert J. Raboteau, eds. *African-American Religion: Interpretive Essays in History and Culture.* New York: Routledge, 1997.

Gardner, William J. *History of Jamaica: From its Discovery by Christopher Columbus to the Present Time, including an account of its Trade and Agriculture.* London: E. Stock, 1873.

Gayle, Clement. *George Liele: Pioneer Missionary to Jamaica.* Kingston, JA: Jamaica Baptist Union, 1982.

BIBLIOGRAPHY

Gibson, William. *Church, State, and Society, 1760-1850*. New York: St. Martin's Press, 1994.
Gilroy, Paul. *Black Atlantic: Modernity and Double-Consciousness*. Cambridge, MA: Harvard University Press 1993.
Glazier, Stephen D. "New World African Ritual: Genuine and Spurious." *Journal for the Scientific Study of Religion* 35.4 (1996) 420-31.
Green, Richard. *John Wesley—Evangelist*. London: The Religious Tract Society, 1905.
Grimes, Ronald. *Deeply Into the Bone: Re-Inventing Rites of Passage*. Berkeley, CA: University of California Press, 2000.
Gordon, Shirley C. *God Almighty Make Me Free: Christianity in Preemancipation Jamaica*. Indianapolis: Indiana University Press, 1996.
———. *Our Cause for His Glory: Christianization and Emancipation in Jamaica*. Kingston, JA: University of the West Indies Press, 1998.
Hempton, David. *Methodism: Empire of the Spirit*. New Haven: Yale University Press, 2005.
Heitzenrater, Richard P. *Mirror and Memory, Reflections on Early Methodism* Nashville: Abingdon, 1989.
———. *The Poor and the People Called Methodists: 1729-1999*. Nashville: Kingswood, 2002.
———. *Wesley and the People Called Methodists*. Nashville: Abingdon, 1995.
Herskovits, Melville J. *Myth of the Negro Past*. New York: Harper & Row, 1941.
Herskovits, Francis S. *Trinidad Village*. New York: Alfred Knopf, 1947.
Hildebrand, Reginald F. *The Times Were Strange and Stirring: Methodist Preachers and the Crisis of Emancipation*. Durham: Duke University Press, 1995.
Hill, Robert. *1826-August 1919*. Vol. 1 of *The Marcus Garvey and UNIA Papers Project*. Los Angeles: University of California at Los Angeles Press, 1995.
Hill, Stephen. *Who's Who in Jamaica, 1919-1920*. Kingston, JA: Gleaner, 1920.
Hindmarsh, D. Bruce. "'My Chains Fell Off, My Heart Was Free' Early Methodist Conversion Narrative in England." *Church History* 68.4 (1999) 910-29.
Holland, Bernard. *Baptism in Early Methodism*. London: Epworth, 1970.
Hylton, Patrick. *Role of Religion in Caribbean History: From Amerindian Shamanism to Rastafarianism*. Washington DC: Morris, 2002.
Inikori, Joseph E., ed. *Forced Migration: The Impact of the Export Slave Trade on African Societies*. London: Hutchinson, 1982.
Jacobson, Matthew F. *Barbarian Virtues: The United States Encounters Foreign Peoples at Home and Abroad, 1876-1917*. New York: Hill and Wang, 2000.
Jenkins, Daniel. "Baptism and Creation." In *Crisis for Baptism: The Report of the 1965 Ecumenical Conference sponsored by the Parish and People Movement*, edited by Basil S. Moss, 95-120. London: SCM LTD, 1965.
Johnson, Charles A. *Frontier Camp Meeting*. Dallas: Southern Methodist University Press, 1955.
Keble, John, and Isaac Walton, eds. *Works of that Learned and Judicious Divine, Mr. Richard Hooker*. Vol. 2. London: Oxford University Press, 1865.
Killingray, David. "The Black Atlantic Missionary Movement and Africa, 1780-1920's." *Journal of Religion in Africa* 33 (2003) 22-30.
Knight, Franklin. *Caribbean: the Genesis of a Fragmented Nationalism*. 2nd ed. New York: Oxford University Press, 1990.
Lampton, Edward W. *Analysis of Baptism*. Nashville: AMEC, 1907.

BIBLIOGRAPHY

Langford, Thomas. "John Wesley's Doctrine of Justification By Faith." *Bulletin of the United Church of Canada Committee on Archives and History* 29 (1980) 55–58.

Lawson, Winston A. *Anglican, Methodist, and Baptist Churches in Jamaica, 1823–1865*. Mona, JA: University of West Indies Press, 1992.

———. *Religion and Race, African and European Roots in Conflict: A Jamaican Testament*. New York: Peter Lang, 1996.

LePage, R. B. *Jamaican Creole*. London: MacMillan, 1960.

Lewis, Gordon K. *Main Currents in Caribbean Thought: The Historical Evolution of Caribbean Society in Its Ideological Aspects, 1492–1900*. Baltimore: John Hopkins University Press, 1983.

Lincoln, C. Eric. *Black Experience in Religion*. New York: Anchor, 1974.

Little, Lawrence S. *Disciples of Liberty: The African Methodist Episcopal Church in the Age of Imperialism, 1884–1916*. Knoxville: University of Tennessee Press, 2000.

Long, Charles H. *Significations: Signs, Symbols, and Images in the Interpretation of Religion*. Aurora: Davies, 1986.

Long, Edward. *History of Jamaica*. Vol. 4. London: Lowndes, 1774.

Mackie, Liz. *The Great Marcus Garvey*. London: Hansib, 2008.

Maddox, Randy. *Responsible Grace*. Nashville: Abingdon, 1994.

Marty, Martin. *Christian World: A Global History*. New York: Modern Library, 2007.

Mbiti, John. *African Religions and Philosophy*. Portsmouth: Heinemann, 1990. Originally published in 1970.

McCollin-Moore, Eustace. "Anglican Meets Spiritual Baptist: A Dialogue with a Religious Other." PhD diss., Columbia Theological Seminary, 2000.

McPherson, James M. "Who Freed the Slaves?" *Proceedings of the American Philosophical Society* 139.1 (1995) 1–10.

Methodist Church in Jamaica, ed. *For Ever Beginning: Two Hundred Years of Methodism in the Western Area*. Kingston, JA: Literature Department of the Methodist Church, 1960.

Mignolo, Walter. *Local Histories/Global Designs: Coloniality, Subaltern Knowledges, and Border Thinking*. Princeton: Princeton University Press, 2000.

Mintz, Sidney. *Sweetness and Power: The Place of Sugar in Modern History*. New York: Penguin, 1986.

Moses, Wilson J. "The Lost World of the Negro, 1895–1919: Black Literary and Intellectual Life before the Renaissance." *Black American Literature Forum* 21.1/2 (1987) 61–84.

Murphy, Joseph M. *Working the Spirit: Ceremonies of the Africa Diaspora*. Boston: Beacon, 1994.

Nettleford, Rex. *Caribbean Cultural Identity: The Case of Jamaica*. Kingston, JA: Ian Randle, 2003.

Norwood, Frederick A. *The Story of American Methodism*. Nashville: Abingdon, 1974.

Outler, Albert. *John Wesley*. New York: Oxford University Press, 1964.

Outler, Albert, and Richard Heitzenrater, eds. *John Wesley's Sermons: An Anthology*. Nashville: Abingdon, 1991.

Padgett, Alan G., ed. *Mission of the Church in Methodist Perspective*. Lewiston: Edwin Mellen, 1992.

Parris, John R. *John Wesley's Doctrine of the Sacraments*. London: Epworth, 1963.

Patterson, Orlando. *Freedom in the Making of Western Culture*. New York: Basic, 1991.

———. *Slavery and Social Death*. Cambridge, MA: Harvard University Press, 1982.

BIBLIOGRAPHY

———. *Sociology of Slavery: An Analysis of the Origins, Development and Structure of Negro Slave Society in Jamaica.* 2nd ed. Kingston, JA: Sangster's, 1973.

Pitts, Walter F. *Old Ship of Zion: The Afro-Baptist Ritual in the African Diaspora.* New York: Oxford University Press, 1993.

Plumb, John H. *England in the Eighteenth Century.* Harmondsworth: Penguin, 1990. Originally published in 1950.

Prince, John W. *Wesley on Religious Education.* New York: The Methodist Book Concern, 1926.

Pugh, Alfred L. *Pioneer Preachers in Paradise: The Legacies of George Liele, Prince Williams and Thomas Paul in Jamaica, the Bahamas and Haiti.* East Peoria: Versa, 2003.

Raboteau, Albert. *Slave Religion.* New York: Oxford University Press, 1978.

Ray, Benjamin C. *African Religions: Symbol, Ritual, and Community.* Upper Saddle River, NJ: Prentice Hall, 2000.

Rieger, Joerg, ed. *Opting for the Margins: Postmodernity and Liberation in Christian Theology.* American Academy of Religion, Reflection and Theory in the Study of Religion. Oxford: Oxford University Press, 2003.

Rivera, Luis N. *A Violent Evangelism: The Political and Religious Conquest of the Americas.* Louisville: Westminster John Knox, 1992.

Rusling, G. W. "A Note on Early Negro Baptist History." *Foundations* 11 (1968) 362–68.

Ruth, Lester. *Early Methodist Life and Spirituality: A Reader.* Nashville: Abingdon, 1998.

Sanneh, Lamin. *Religion and the Variety of Culture: A Study in Origin and Practice.* Valley Forge: Trinity Press International, 1996.

———. *Translating the Message: The Missionary Impact on Culture.* Maryknoll, NY: Orbis, 1989.

Schensul, Stephen, et al., eds. *Essential Ethnographic Methods: Observations, Interviews and Questionnaires.* Walnut Creek, CA: AltaMira, 1999.

Schuler, Monica. "Myalism and the African Religious Tradition in Jamaica." In *Africa and the Caribbean: The Legacies of a Link*. edited by Margaret Crahan and Franklin Knight, 65–79. Baltimore: John Hopkins University Press, 1979.

Semmel, Bernard. *The Methodist Revolution.* New York: Basic, 1973.

Simpson, George, E. "The Acculturative Process in Jamaican Revivalism." In *Fifth International Congress of Anthropological and Ethnological Sciences, September 1–9, 1956,* edited by Anthony F. C. Wallace, 332–41. Philadelphia: University of Pennsylvania Press, 1960.

———. "The Nine Night Ceremony in Jamaica." *The Journal of American Folklore* 70.278 (1957) 329–35.

Sobel, Mechal. *Trabelin' On: The Slave Journey to an Afro-Baptist Faith.* Westport, CT: Greenwood, 1978.

Somé, Malidoma. *Of Water and the Spirit: Ritual, Magic and Initiation in the Life of an African Shaman.* New York: Penguin Books, 1994.

———. *Ritual: Power, Healing, and Community.* New York: Penguin, 1997.

Smith, C. S. *History of the African Methodist Episcopal Church 1856–1922.* Vol. 2. Philadelphia: AMEC, 1922.

Smith, Timothy. "Historical Waves of Religious Interest in America." *The Annals of the American Academy of Political and Social Science* 332 (1960) 9–19.

Smith, Warren Thomas. *John Wesley and Slavery.* Nashville: Abingdon, 1986.

Stamm, Mark Wesley. *Let Every Soul Be Jesus' Guest: A Theology of the Open Table.* Nashville: Abingdon, 2006.

BIBLIOGRAPHY

Starkey, Lycurgus. *Work of the Holy Spirit: A Study in Wesleyan Theology.* Nashville: Abingdon Press, 1962.

Starkie, Andrew. "Contested Histories of the English Church: Gilbert Burnet and Jeremy Collier." *Huntington Library Quarterly* 68.1–2 (2005) 335–51.

Stewart, Dianne M. *Three Eyes for the Journey: African Dimensions of the Jamaican Religious Experience.* New York: Oxford University Press, 2005.

Stewart, Robert. *Religion and Society in Postemancipation Jamaica.* Knoxville: University of Tennessee Press, 1992.

Stookey, Laurence H. *Baptism: Christ's Act in the Church.* Nashville: Abingdon, 1982.

Talbot, Frederick H. *African American Worship: New Eyes for Seeing.* Little Rock: Fairway Press, 1998.

Tounouga, Camille T. "The Symbolic Function of Water in Sub-Saharan Africa: A Cultural Approach." *Leonardo* 36.4 (2003) 283.

Turner, Henry M. "Letter to The American Colonization Society." *African Repository* 1.2 (1875) 39.

Turner, Mary. *Slaves and Missionaries: The Disintegration of Jamaican Slave Society, 1787–1834.* Kingston, JA: University of West Indies Press, 1998.

Vickers, John A. *Journals of Dr. Thomas Coke.* Nashville: Abingdon, 2005.

Waddell, Rev. Hope. *Twenty Nine Years in the West Indies and Central Africa.* London: Frank Cass, 1970. Originally published 1863.

Walker, Clarence E. *Rock in a Weary Land: The African Methodist Episcopal Church during the Civil War and Reconstruction.* Baton Rouge: Louisiana State University Press, 1982.

Wesley, Charles. *March 9, 1736 to December 28, 1747.* Vol. 1 of *Journal of Charles Wesley.* London: John Mason, 1849. Reprint. Grand Rapids: Baker, 1980.

Wesley, Susanna. *Susanna Wesley: The Complete Writings.* Edited by Charles Wallace, Jr. Oxford: Oxford University Press, 1997.

Whitefield, George. *George Whitefield's Journals.* London: Billing and Sons Limited, Guildford and London, 1960.

Williams, Joseph. *Voodoos and Obeahs: Phases of West Indian Witchcraft.* New York: Dial, 1932.

Williams, Lewin L. *Caribbean Theology.* New York: Peter Lang, 1994.

Williams, T. G. *Methodist and Anglicanism in the Light of Scripture and History.* Toronto: Publishing Company, 1888.

Wilmour, Gayraud. *Black Radicalism and Black Religion.* Maryknoll, NY: Orbis, 1998.

Wright, R. R., Jr. *Sixteenth Episcopal District of the African Methodist Episcopal Church.* Nashville: AMEC, 1964.

Wright-Hayre, Ruth. *Tell Them We Are Rising: A Memoir of Faith in Education.* New York: John Wiley & Sons, 1997.

Young, Jason R. *Rituals of Resistance: African Atlantic Religion in Kongo and the Low Country South in the Era of Slavery.* Baton Rouge: Louisiana State University Press, 2007.

INDEX OF NAMES

Abraham 106
Adam 105
Allen, Jr. Ernest 178
Allen, Richard 9, 37, 41, 42, 44, 45, 67, 162, 170, 183
Alley, Mary 40
Alexander, Jeffrey C. 149, 152, 1977
Alleyne, Mervyn 14, 50, 51, 53, 54, 58, 59, 65
Angell, Stephen 164, 166, 177
Asbury, Francis 40, 41, 44
Augustine 101
Austin-Broos, Diane 17, 18, 188, 189, 190, 191

Baillie, D.M. 102, 109
Bailey, W.T. Rev. (Old Harbour) 183, 185, 191, 192, 194
Baker, Moses 75, 80, 81, 82, 83
Barrett, W.J. 151
Bastide, Roger 61
Bay, Edna G. 62, 63
Beckerlegge, Oliver 149
Beckwith, Marsha Warren 185, 186, 188, 189
Bedward, Alexander 8, 16, 186, 187, 189, 190
Berry, L.L. 192
Bhaba, Homi 23
Bilby, Kenneth 54
Bisnauth, Dale 65, 69
Bleby, Henry 132, 135, 158
Bloch, Maurice 20, 24

Borgen, Ole 6, 12, 105, 106, 116, 117, 118, 119, 121
Boukman 65
Braithwaite, Edward Kamau 4, 9, 59
Bridge, Donald 100
Bridges, George Wilson 157, 158
Brooks, A.A. 187
Bryan, Hugh 74
Bryan, Jonathan 74
Buchner, J.H. 71
Bunting, Jabez 44
Burchell, Thomas 129
Bynum, Cornelius 170

Campbell, Sophia 40
Campbell, Ted 6, 13, 31, 32, 33, 107, 118, 147, 196
Campbell, Thomas 33
Cannon, William 116
Charles I 26
Chase, Salmon 175
Chevannes, Barry 81, 190
Chilcote, Paul 32, 92, 93
Cho, John C. 105
Clarke, John 43
Coke, Thomas 40, 42, 43, 125
Colón, Christobal 68
Cone, James 151
Cooke, Stephen 75
Cooper, Terry D. 153
Corlett, John 139, 140, 144
Cornelius 99
Cornish, John 47
Cox, Francis 129, 130

INDEX OF NAMES

Crahan, Margaret 88
Cromwell, Oliver 69
Cuffy 65
Curnock, Nicholas 7
Curtin, Phillip 7, 14, 15, 48, 84, 88, 91, 129, 134, 157

Davies, Rupert E. 31
Derrick, W.B. 166, 167
Dickerson, Dennis 46
Dimond, Sydney 38
Disney, Richard R. 163
Dorrien, Gary 170
DuBois, W.E.B. 50, 181, 182
Dumar, Alfonso 22, 122, 149, 162, 167, 169, 171–74, 177–80, 183, 184, 191, 192, 193, 194, 195, 197
Duncan, Peter 85, 86, 127

Edmondson, Jr., John 144
Edwards, Bryan 53, 64, 65
Erskine, Noel 76
Ethiopian eunuch 96

Febvre, Lucian 24
Felton, Gayle 6, 13, 112, 113, 114, 115, 118
Ferguson, Everett 101, 119
Field, M.J. 59
Findlay, George G. 125, 126, 139, 141
Finn, Thomas 20
Finney, Charles 9, 17, 89
Foster, George 50
Fountain, William A. 194
Foy, Captain 28
Frazier, E. Franklin 51
Fulop, Timothy 50

Galphin, George 74
Gardner, W.J. 18, 92
Garvey, Marcus Mosiah 10, 178, 179, 181, 187
Gayle, Clement 79, 80
Gibb, George 75, 83
Gilbert, Nathaniel 40
Glazier, Stephen 156

Goddard, Terry Dale 170
Gordon, Shirley 7, 9, 15, 17, 130, 131, 142, 154
Green, Richard 30
Grimes, R.L. 152

Hammett, William 43, 125
Hayes, Rutherford, 164, 165
Heitzenrater, Richard 29, 37, 120, 121
Hempton, David 6, 13, 39, 121
Herskovits, Frances 155
Herskovits, M.J. 7, 14, 50, 51, 142, 143, 155
Hill, Stephen 172
Hill, Robert A. 178, 179
Hill, William 125
Hindmarsh, D. Bruce 154
Hollar, G.J. 47
Holdsworth, William W. 125
Holland, Bernard 6, 12, 117, 118, 120
Hollar, G.J. Rev. (Riversdale) 47, 183
Hooker, Richard 114
Hoosier, "Black Harry" 41
Hudson, Winthrop 51
Hughes, Langston 19
Hurst, John 191, 192
Hylton, Kitty 158

Inikori, Joseph 48

Jacobson, Matthew F. 169
Jenkins, Daniel 106
Jesus of Nazareth 94
Jesus the Christ 94, 96
Johnson, Charles A. 28, 41
Jordan, Edward 133, 137

Keble, John 114
Kerr, David 139, 145, 146
Killingray, David 168
Kirkland, Colonel 73
Knight, Franklin 88
Kreider, Alan 20

Lampton, Edward W. 184
Langford, Thomas 108
Lawson, Winston 143

INDEX OF NAMES

Lee, Robert E. 175
LePage, Robert 48, 53
Leslie, C. 69
Lewis, George 75
Lewis, Gordon 1, 7, 14
Liele, George 21, 72, 73, 74, 75, 77, 78, 79, 81, 82, 83, 93, 154, 156, 158, 159, 160, 191, 195, 197
Lincoln, Abraham 176
Little, Lawrence 21, 22
Locke, Alaine 170, 180, 181, 182
Locke, John 26
Long, Charles 7, 68, 123
Long, Edward 58, 65, 69
Luther, Martin 116
Lydia 99
Lynch, Bishop 69

Mackie, Liz 180
Maddox, Randy 20, 103, 104, 112
Mann, Kristin 62
Marty, Martin 31
Martyr, Justin 100, 101
Maxfield, Thomas 30
Mbiti, John 7, 14, 48, 51, 57
McPherson, James M. 176
McTyeire, Holland 28
Mignolo, Walter 22
Mintz, Sidney 50, 51
McCollin-Moore, Eustace 156
Mveng, Englebert 151
Morris, Calvin 170
Moses, Wilson J. 174, 177
Moss, Basil S. 106

Nazrey, Willis 163
Nettleford, Rex 4, 9

Origen 101
Outler, Albert 37, 115, 119

Padgett, Alan 147
Palmer, A. Mitchell 180
Palmer, Phoebe 9, 17, 90
Palmer, Waitstill 74
Parrinder, Geoffrey 54

Parris, John 6, 12, 107, 117
Patterson, Orlando 21, 48, 49, 52, 53, 59, 61, 63, 69, 70, 77, 131, 132, 150
Patterson, Rev. (Temple Hall) 183
Paul 97, 99, 131
Payne, Daniel 45, 46, 47, 175, 177
Pearson, or Pierson, W.B. 22, 171, 183, 192
Pennock, Thomas 19, 122, 123, 124, 125, 128, 129, 132, 133, 135, 136, 137, 138, 139, 140, 141, 142, 144, 145, 146, 147, 148, 149, 150
Philip the Disciple 9
Phillipo, James 59
Phypers, David 100
Pitts, Walter F. 157
Plumb, J.H. 27
Price, Richard 50, 51
Prince, John W. 110
Pugh, Alfred L. 79

Raboteau, Albert 61, 123
Rankin, J.W. 171, 177, 180, 191, 192, 193
Ransom, Reverdy 170
Rattenbury, J. Ernest 6, 12
Ray, Benjamin 7, 14
Rieger, Joerg 23
Rippon, Colonel 74, 81
Roosevelt, Teddy 169
Rowden, Mr. 138
Rowe, John 81, 82
Rufinus 101
Rusling, G.W. 159
Ruth, Lester 34

Sanneh, Lamin 170
Sapir, Edward 156
Seaga, Edward 160
Schaeffer, C.T. 171
Schuler, Monica 87, 88
Sharpe, Henry 73
Sharpe, Samuel 129, 130, 131, 144, 161
Simpson, George E. 62, 186

145

INDEX OF NAMES

Silas 99
Smith, C.S. 163, 180, 193
Smith, Timothy 8, 17, 18
Sobel, Mechal 76
Somé, Malidoma 57, 151, 152
Spence, T.H. 183
Spurgeon, C.H. 90
Starkey, Lycurgus 38
Starkie, Andrew 26
Stevens, Thaddeus 175
Stewart, Benjamin 163
Stewart, Dianne 8, 15, 22, 53, 54, 66, 130
Stewart, Robert 135, 137, 143, 151
Stearn, Shubal 74
Sumner, Charles 175
Sutliff, Mary 127, 128
Swigle, Thomas Nicholas 79

Tacky 65
Talbot, Frederick H. 45
Tanner, Benjamin 46, 47
Tounouga, Camille 186, 187
Turner, Henry McNeal 163–67, 175, 176, 177
Turner, Mary 129, 131
Tyerman, Luke 117

Wade, Ben 175
Waddell, Hope Masterson 59, 82, 83
Walker, Clarence E. 176
Wall, William 104
Wallace, Jr. Charles 110
Walters, Mr. 138

Walton, Isaac 114
Ward, T.E. 138
Ward, Valentine 140, 141, 144
Warren, Samuel 149
Warrener, William 43
Watson, Kevin 29
Wesley, Charles 2, 28, 30, 33, 34, 35, 36
Wesley, John 2, 8, 16, 17, 19, 20, 23, 26–30, 32–34, 37, 38, 42, 44, 74, 82, 94, 101, 103, 104, 105, 107–17, 119, 120–22, 124, 128, 47, 196
Wesley, Samuel 104, 119
Wesley, Susanna 30, 109, 110, 119
Whitefield, George 4, 26, 27, 28, 29, 72, 82, 93
Whitehouse, Isaac 139
Whittier, John Greenleaf 171
Wilberforce, William 157
Williams, F.E. 67
Williams, Joseph 65, 66
Williams, Rev. (Morant Bay) 183
Williams, T.G. 116, 117
Wilmour, Gayraud 165
Wilson, Woodrow 170
Wright, Sr., R.R. 171
Wright, Jr., R.R. 171, 194
Wright-Hayre, Ruth 171
Wood, Leonard 169

Young, G.L. Rev. (Brown's Hall) 191
Young, Jason 2, 51

Zele, Adam 7, 13

www.ingramcontent.com/pod-product-compliance
Lightning Source LLC
Chambersburg PA
CBHW071506150426
43191CB00009B/1434